MW00415907

AWAKENING

FROM OZ

A Path to Enlightenment
in a Paradoxical Universe

by David Panozzo

OBODONI PRESS
Chicago, Illinois

Obodoni Press
P.O. Box 409036
Chicago, Illinois 60640-9036
Printed in the United States of America

First printing 1997.

10 9 8 7 6 5 4 3 2 1

Library of Congress Cataloging-in-Publication Data
Panozzo, David
Awakening From Oz : A Path to Enlightenment in a Paradoxical Universe
Includes bibliographical references.
ISBN 0-9656556-5-2

97-91553
   CIP

*Cover artwork and design
by Todd Nguyen*

DEDICATION

To God, my Father, for without your love I know I would not be.

ACKNOWLEDGMENTS

I want to thank my loving partner David. You have shown me the truth of what a relationship based in love is all about. Without your unending love and support this book would not have been written. I want to thank my family for their wonderful support. Your love gives me the security and confidence to be the person I am today. I want to thank all the many writers for their loving words that helped me to find my way home. Especially, I would like to thank Ken Carey, Jane Roberts, and Neale Donald Walsch. Your books took my level of understanding to new heights. I want to thank all the wonderful artists whose music has touched my soul, with a special thanks to Desree and Annie Lennox. Your music spirited the writing of this book. And finally I want to thank Peter Kime and Natalie Holden. Your editing of this book helped it to become the book it was meant to be.

I love you all and thank you for your love and your wisdom.

CONTENTS

INTRODUCTION

This book is written as a response to a promise I made with God. As a young boy sitting in the chair in my bedroom, I agreed to do his work here on earth. I remember it as if it were yesterday. I agreed to do this work with two conditions: first, I wanted to lead a "normal" life, and second, I did not want to be considered a "weirdo." Many people have paved the road before me, making what I have written much more easily accepted and the possibility of your accepting it as your truth that much greater. To all those who have come before me I am eternally grateful. What I have written in this book is nothing new. There is nothing that has not been said before thousands of times in many different ways since the beginning of time. Truth is truth. However, I have attempted to write this book in accordance with today's thinking. When dealing with a topic such as God and his relationship to humanity, I wanted to do it with an approach that was not so anthropomorphic. One of our greatest barriers to knowing God is that we endow God with human characteristics.

In today's scientific and technological society things seem to be getting easier and, at the same time, much more complex. I wanted to use terms that could be understood and interpreted by everyone. I awoke one day with the insight of using the properties of the numbers of zero and one and their relationship to each other as the way to explain God, humanity, and the relationship God has to humanity. I was delighted to find out during the writing of this book that computers are also based on a binary or two-number system. How appropriate. Even our technological advancements can be used to express spiritual truths, although computers will not be discussed in this book. Also, I have used the basic concept of relativity as the way to explain the design of our universe. It is when we understand who God is and our relationship to this force that we can consciously use this earthly existence for its intended purpose.

The Wizard of Oz, one of the most popular and well loved movies, can be seen as an analogy for the enlightenment process. I compare the process outlined in this book to Dorothy's journey to the land of Oz in the hopes that you can recognize her journey as your journey here on earth.

On one level none of the information in this book is mine. It is the culmination of the thoughts and ideologies of many different people and cultures. On another level the information is all mine because I am this book. This book is the result of my years of intense study and personal experiences with God. Throughout my life I have been guided to material that helped me explain what I had experienced. It is with this intention that I write this book so that you may gain greater clarity and understanding of your life and your experiences. It is very important to the success of the process described in this book that you do not deny or label any experiences that you had or will have as fiction or fantasy. Do not try to explain away any seemingly unexplainable events in your life by denying that they happened or that they were just a figment of your imagination. This is why I do not include any personal experiences and was hesitant to put examples in this book. I did not want you to try to recreate my experiences or to be influenced by the examples. I feel it is much more valuable that you apply this information to your own life in any way you feel is appropriate. The focus of this book is not to give you answers. You already have the answers. What I am trying to do is help you open yourself up to a grander vision of yourself and have you look at your life and your experiences in a different way. My vision in writing this book is for you to reclaim your power as a creative, loving, powerful being and to trust yourself enough to stop looking outside yourself for answers that only you have.

It has been my desire since a young boy to be one with God and to be of service to others. I have been saying a prayer every day since I first agreed to do God's work. I would like to share it with you now.

Oh, Father,

Father of Light and Love.

Show me the way.

Help me to find my way back to you

and allow me to help others along my journey.

Give me the strength I need to be an instrument for you

here on this earth and let thy will be done.

I still have no clear idea of exactly how this work I agreed to do will be carried out. I only hope that in some way this book can help you find the truth you seek and help you to live a more peaceful, loving, joyful, and abundant life.

PREFACE

I want to start off by saying that you need not fear your enlightenment. Do not hear these words mentally but feel the words. Breathe in these words and allow them to speak to the core of your being. The fear of our atonement is what is keeping us from achieving it more than anything else. Look beyond the words contained on the pages of this book. Words are symbols and as such can never convey truth. Seek the spirit of these words. It is through spirit that truth is revealed.

If you think you have chosen to read this book by accident, then you do not understand how the universe works. However, I know I did not have to tell you that. The people that will be guided to this book are the people who have been preparing themselves for it. Even if you do not acknowledge it, you have been on this path for many years, for many lifetimes.

This book is **a** path to enlightenment not, **the** path. There are many roads that lead us back to a reunion with our creator. It was my intent in writing this book to keep it as short and simple as possible. There are volumes of books on topics on which I spend only a few pages. I believe that you will be familiar with much of the material. My focus is to highlight and elevate your understanding of what you already know. My goal is to take all of your knowledge and experiences and formulate them into a logical, cohesive system of thought that has practical value in your everyday life. However, even if you have very little exposure to material such as this or none at all, this book will give you a solid foundation from which you can continue your search.

One of the most important prerequisites to obtaining the most benefit from reading this book is to keep an open heart and an open mind. You must be willing to consider the possibility of a truth other than the one you currently know before the truth of your existence can be revealed to you. It is important for you to temporarily put aside all of your beliefs and leave yourself open to the information contained within this book. If you allow yourself to feel the truth of these words, then the truth will make itself known to you. I am not here to argue or convince anyone as to what is truth. Truth needs no argument.

This book is written like a house is built, one brick at a time. To have a weak brick is to jeopardize the integrity of the whole house. Each chapter is built upon the preceding chapter, so to read on when you do not understand what you have just read will weaken the understanding of the whole process.

Remembering also plays a very important part in the reading of this book. It is important when reading each chapter that you incorporate the information from all the preceding chapters. To leave out any part in this process of trying to understand the whole can lead to a distortion of the information and a misunderstanding of the message of this book. I leave reminders in chapters where I feel some misunderstanding may take place. I have intentionally used the word "God" to refer to our Higher Self because in our society the term "God" is ingrained with certain character-istics and meaning for all of us. It is important to this process that we come to grips with this term and not try to ignore its relevancy in our lives by replacing it with other terms. Also, I continually flip flop the pronouns I associate with the term "God" as a way to help you to expand your concept of who and what God is.

I suggest you read this book through one time. If the information feels good and rings true for you, then I suggest that you keep rereading this book until you receive no new insights and you can say that the information contained within it has become a part of you.

It is my prayer for this book that it shifts your search for God and meaning in your life from a purely mental process to an experiential process of the heart. Then I hope you will have the courage and the confidence to go out and teach all that you know and express the love that you are, in what-ever joyful expression it may take.

Now that we are in the midst of returning to a love-based reality, it is important that you choose to remember and accept who you are. It is time to reclaim your power as a creative being and express the love that is you.

PART I

DEFINING GOD

CHAPTER 0

THE GOD CONCEPT

To define God is to limit God.
To limit God is to not know God.
To not know God is to fear God.

God is the most misunderstood force in the universe. God is many things to many people. Dorothy's concept of God, the mysterious Wizard, exists in the minds of many people within the Judeo-Christian tradition and is the most commonly held view of God in our society today. God is imagined as a masculine energy with an ethereal human-like body. God is thought of as an all-powerful, all-knowing, all-seeing spirit that is to be feared. God is seen as some sort of scorekeeper. He keeps a record of everything we do. He then hands down punishments and blessings based on our actions. At the end of our life he tallies up our deeds and decides if we are to join him in heaven, be sent to hell with Satan, or live in purgatory, a sort of holding tank for marginal cases.

These ideas could not be any further from the truth. God is not a human-like figure with human characteristics. She would not take on such a limited form. God's form is formless and thus indescribable. It would be better to think of

God as an energy source such as electricity. We can not see electricity, but we know it exists. We know it exists because of our experiences with it. It is difficult to describe what electricity is without relating it to its effects. Electricity is the force that causes a bulb to light or a machine to run. In this same way, it is difficult to explain God in any way other than through the relationship that God has to us personally and the world we live in. However, what I wanted to do was to find a less subjective relationship between two simple and familiar concepts that could be used to provide greater understanding of who God is and what our relationship is to this being. I have found such a relationship to be contained within mathematics.

One way to understand God is through the properties of the number zero. God has the same characteristics as the number zero, and his relationship to humanity is comparable to the relationship that the number zero has to all numbers. Thus, one way in which we can better understand and know God is by examining the mathematical properties of zero. I want to make it clear that I am not trying here to put forth a scientific explanation of God. I am metaphysically interpreting mathematical concepts and their relationship to one another as an analogy to God and his relationship to humanity, as a way for us to gain greater clarity and unity surrounding the nature of God and our relationship to this force.

First, let's start by examining the symbol for zero, the circle "0." When looking at a circle we do not know where it starts or where it ends. When we draw a circle, the starting point is also the ending point, and the ending point is the starting point. They are the same. If its point of origin and its point of completion are the same, it has no beginning or ending. Just as the circle has no beginning or ending, God has no beginning or ending. God is infinite and eternal.

Second, on a number line the number zero is the starting point for all numbers positive or negative. Any other number only exists in its relationship to zero. One is only one because it is one more than zero, ten is ten because it is ten more than zero, one trillion is one trillion because it is one trillion more than zero. Perhaps numbers should be written as 0-1, or 0-10, or 0-1,000,000,000,000 to denote their relationships to zero, because without zero no other number can exist. So if God is as zero, without God nothing else can exist.

Third, zero raised to the zero power is undefined.[1] The reason it is undefined is because zero is an unlimited number, and it is impossible to define something that is unlimited. I know in mathematics that zero is defined as the empty set but rather than the absence of any number, think of zero as the sum total of all possible numbers combined. This is how zero will be defined throughout this book. Zero does contain nothing, but in that nothing is contained everything. When we break down nothing into its two component words we have "no" and "thing." When we state we

---

[1] The power to which a number is raised is the number of times the number multiplies or extends itself out. For example, 2 raised to the fourth power is written as 2^4 which stands for 2 x 2 x 2 x 2 or 16.

are "no-thing," we are actually saying we are not one particular thing. At the same time, if we are not one particular thing, we have the potential to be anything, and that potential already includes everything that exists. "Nothing" then actually includes everything in existence and the unlimited possibilities that have yet to exist. Like zero, God is no-thing, or rather everything and the potential to be anything. God encompasses all things. As it is impossible to define zero, it is impossible to define God. We can see that to define God is an impossibility because to define God is to limit God. A limited God is not God. God is everything that was, is, and will be. God is everything seen and unseen and everything known and unknown. God is unlimited possibilities or, as Deepak Chopra has termed it, "Pure Potentiality."

Fourth, zero is neither positive or negative. It has no opposites. So like zero, anything that is considered to have polarity is not God. That is why in God there is no good or evil, nor right or wrong. God is neither male or female nor anything else dualistic. God exists in a state of non-duality. God just is.

In summary, God is the eternal energy force, the force of unlimited possibilities that exists in a state of non-duality through which all else exists and is made possible.

CHAPTER 0 - 1

GOD AS LOVE

The only way to know love is to experience love.
The only way to experience love is to know God.
The only way to know God is through the experience of love.

Since God by definition can not be defined then how can we know God? God is not defined. God is experienced. Can joy be defined without relating it to an experience? Can joy be held in the palm of our hand? Does joy exist? We know joy exists because we have experienced it in the birth of a new baby, or in the embrace of a lover's arms. It is through these experiences that we know joy exists and we define for ourselves what joy is. As the only way to know joy is through experience, the only way to know God is through experience. In all religious and spiritual philosophies, at least the ones I am familiar with, God is defined as love. God and love are synonymous. When we experience love, we are experiencing God. It is through the experience of love that we come to know and define for ourselves who God is and develop a relationship with this energy. However, love is an inner experience and thus a subjective and different experience for each person. This makes it impossible for us to know for sure that the experience we are defining as love is the exact same experience that other people are defining as love. Are the experiences that cause us to feel loved the same experiences that causes everyone to feel loved? Is it a valid assumption to believe that love can only be evidenced through specific actions and specific experiences? Is it correct for us to believe that every person will react to all similar experiences with the same emotional and physical response? Even though we like to label certain actions and experiences as either loving or non-loving, is it valid to try to fit the experience of love into a specific range of actions and experiences so we can define it? Just because we do not view an act or experience as an expression of love, does that make the act intrinsically a non-loving act? If someone else views what we consider to be a non-loving act as an act of love, does this then make the act an act of love?

As we can see, there is much confusion surrounding the experience of love and what it means to be loving. The concept of love, as it exists within the context of the universe, is not love as it is understood in our society today.[2] It is not only the love that is the subject of books, plays, movies, poetry, and song. It is not only the love that is evidenced in the love you feel for a lover or a child. As humans, we believe we fall in love. This implies that love is something that happens to us. This also implies it is something we give, and if we can give it, then we can also

---

[2] When I use the term universe or universal throughout this text, I mean the way something exists by design or as God created it, not how we have come to interpret it. I am referring to its function in all experiences because this physical experience is just one of an infinite number of experiences which make up the totality of the universe.

withhold it and take it away. We believe we can be in love with another person and then three years later no longer love that person. As parents we believe we love our children and then we can we stop loving them because we discover they are homosexual or because they have murdered someone. However, if God equals love, then love contains the same characteristics as God. Love is eternal and unlimited. Love can not fade away. Love can not suddenly cease to exist. Does this mean that the act of divorcing someone or the rejection of a child because of their homosexuality or their murderous act is an expression of love?

If we believe God is love, then love is all God is. God's love can not be withheld. God's love can not be given and then taken away. Just as without God nothing else could exist, without love nothing else could exist. Love is the reason for every action and experience in the universe. No matter how God chooses to express itself, each action and experience is an expression of love. Since love is an inner experience, the love energy originates from within each one of us and not outside of ourselves. This is why to know love and thus know God there can be only be one person who we must love, within the context of the universe, and that is **ourselves**. If we do not know what it is to love ourselves we can not possibly know what it is to love another. It is through loving ourselves that the possibility exists that we can love another.

As previously stated, because love is an abstract concept, the only way to know love is through our experiences with it. Since the experience of love is personal and will be a different experience for each person, I sought to find a neutral way of explaining the parameters of this subjective experience. Once again, such an analogy exists within the realm of mathematics.

In mathematics, any number raised to the zero power is one.[3] That is, any number multiplied by itself zero times is equal to and has the same properties as the number one. A number, in the context of this book, represents everything that exists, both seen and unseen. A number raised to the zero power expresses its essence or true nature, because to multiply a number zero times is not to multiply it at all. Also, since God is represented by zero, zero power defines how God expresses or evidences its power. In being raised to the zero power, a number expresses its God essence or true nature, as God chooses to express its power or the magnificence of its being. Since God is as zero, which encompasses all things, and any number raised to the zero power, which is the way God expresses its power, equals one, one will be the mathematical representation of love, because God is love. Therefore, any number, which represents all things seen and unseen, raised to the zero power, which represents its true nature, is love. Even though outwardly everyone and everything appear different, the true nature of everything is love.

---

[3] Zero power is defined as the value of any real number except zero raised to the zero power is always 1. Any number except zero with the exponent of zero is equal to 1. For example, $3^0 = 1$

Now that love is analogous with the number one, to better understand the experience of God as love, we need to examine the mathematical properties of the number one.

Thus far we have stated that love has a dual role: 1) it is the essence of all things, and 2) it is the way God expresses its being. To have a complete definition of love we must incorporate both of these aspects into our definition. We will start defining love by characterizing the nature of the love experience. It is the multiplication and division properties of one that best describe the nature of this experience.

First, any number multiplied by one equals itself. For example, one times ten equals ten. Through the multiplication property of one we can see that one is a number that does not enhance another number. Since one or love is how God expresses itself, love is an experience where the object of the love is allowed to exist as it was created.

Second, any number divided by one remains that same number. For example, ten divided by one equals ten. Through the division property of one we can see that one is a number that does not destroy another number. It allows the number to remain the same. Again, God expresses itself as love through an experience where the object of the love is allowed to exist as it was created.

So love is an experience in which the object of the love is allowed to exist as it was created. Love by design does not try to change or alter the object of its love.

Even though love is an inner experience or feeling, this experience is expressed through outward actions. It is the addition and subtraction properties of the number one that describe the concrete experiences which demonstrate the experience of love.

To start, if we add one to any number, it increases that number by one. For example, nine plus one equals ten. Ten is one more than nine. In action, one is an additive or positive experience. Since one is how God expresses itself as love, love is evidenced by those actions we consider positive or good. I understand that what we consider good or positive is subjectively determined, and the way that we choose to express goodness can be different for each person. However, what I am referring to here are those actions and experiences that have been traditionally considered in this society as being admirable and desirable. Some examples are providing aid to the less fortunate and giving birth to a new baby.

Next, if we subtract one from any number, it decreases that number by one. For example, ten minus one equals nine. Nine is less than ten. In action, one is also a subtractive or negative experience. Since one is analogous to how God expresses itself as love, the experience of love is also evidenced by those actions we consider negative or bad. By negative or bad I am referring to those actions and experiences which have been traditionally consider in this society as wrong and unwanted, such as killing and illness.

So all actions that we do, or that are done to us, whether we consider them as positive or negative experiences, are loving experiences of God.

Finally, on a number line one is the first whole number to the right of zero. One is a positive number. As a feeling experience, love is positive. Love is the feeling of joy. Joy, as it is defined within the context of the universe and as it will be used in this book, is not joy as we traditionally think of it. It is not only joy as Webster's dictionary defines it, "A feeling of delight; happiness; gladness." It is best understood as it is defined by Emmanuel in *Emmanuel's Book* as "experiencing without pain." The universal concept of joy has to do with how we view our life experiences and not with the content of the experiences. Joy is experiencing all of life as positive, regardless of the circumstances.

Just as zero encompasses all things, love encompasses all emotions. Love is not the experience of a single emotion but the sum total of all emotions. Love is a process where through our emotions, in union with our mind, we create an entire array of experiences. Through these experiences we then define for ourselves what love is. So it is important to understand that it is by design that we experience all emotions, otherwise there would be no way for us to know love. As without God nothing else could exist, so it is that without love nothing else could exist. Remember, love existed before our experience of it. Love is not the result of experience, it is the cause.

To sum it up, love is a process—a process through which our personal experience of God, our joy, is neither enhanced or diminished by any act or action.

CHAPTER 0 - 2

THE ILLUSION OF SEPARATION

If God is no-thing,
then how can there be less than no-thing?
If God is everything,
then how can there be more than everything?
It is impossible to separate from that which is both
no-thing and everything.

Many stories have been created around our supposed separation from God, the most common being the Biblical story of Adam and Eve and the Garden of Eden. As the story goes, Man, God, and nature all lived together in perfect harmony until the day Adam and Eve decided to eat the fruit from the forbidden tree. God, angry at them for eating the apple, banished the two from Eden. They had sinned. They were cursed to live out the rest of their lives separate from God. To punish them, he condemned them to lead a life of pain and struggle. Through their struggle they could atone for their horrible sin and one day be reunited with God and allowed to return to the Garden. The only truth to this story is in its concept of heaven and hell. Heaven is the experience of feeling united with God, our creator. Hell is the experience of feeling separate from God, our creator. The garden is a metaphor: heaven and hell are not places; they are states of mind.

It is impossible to separate ourselves from God. We can not separate ourselves from something that is everything. The separation we feel is an illusion and can be best illustrated through the multiplication and division properties of zero and through the relationship that the number one has to all numbers.

In mathematics, when zero is multiplied by itself or any number and when any number is multiplied by zero, the answer is zero. For example, $0 \times 0 = 0$, $0 \times 4 = 0$ and $4 \times 0 = 0$. When we multiply numbers, the result we attain represents the sum total of the number of times a number is added to itself. For example, $2 \times 4 = 8$ is representative of $2 + 2 + 2 + 2 = 8$. So in this context we can see that $0 \times 0 = 0$ is representative of $0 + 0 = 0$ and $0 \times 4 = 0$ is representative of $0 + 0 + 0 + 0 = 0$. However, when we reverse the equation and multiply 4×0 and still the answer is zero, the explanation is not so clear. Since zero is defined as the sum total of all possible numbers, when any number is multiplied by zero, the sum total of this multiplication would already be included within zero; therefore the answer is zero. Remember, all possible numbers are already included as a part of zero, so multiplying a number by zero is the same as adding a part of zero to itself. Therefore, 4 (which is already included in zero) $\times 0 = 0$ can be translated into $0 + 0 = 0$. So, if God is as zero, it would be impossible for anything to exist outside of or separate from God, because God encompasses all things.

There are three possibilities for using zero in a division equation: 1) we can take zero and divide it by a number other than zero; 2) we can take any number and divide it by zero; and 3) we can take zero and divide it by itself. The result of any division is obtained through the multiplication of the number we are dividing with by another number, which is usually an unknown. For example, $4 \div 2 = ?$ means $4 = 2 \times ?$. The answer is 2 because $2 \times 2 = 4$. With this in mind, let us begin by examining the first of these three possibilities, zero divided by any number other than zero. This equation can be written as $0 \div a = b$. This means that $0 = a \times b$. This equation is asking, "What number (a), which is any number other than 0, when multiplied by (b) is equal to 0?" The mathematical explanation is as follows: since (a) is any number other than 0 then (b) must be zero, because in order for the answer to be zero, one of the numbers must be zero. However, based on our definition of zero, it would be impossible for the combination of any two numbers to be equal to zero because zero is the sum total of all possible numbers and therefore an infinite number. Any combination of numbers multiplied together is going to be a part of zero but not the sum total of zero. Therefore, 0 must be the answer for (b) to encompass (a) as a part of zero. So the reason 0 divided by any number other than 0 is 0 is because zero can not be divided. Since God is like zero, God can not be divided because God is everything. Nothing that exists can ever exist separate from God.

Next, zero divided by itself is undetermined. It is un-determined because $0 \div 0 = b$ means $0 = 0 \times b$, and since any number times 0 equals 0, (b) could be any number and thus can not be determined. As we relate this to our interpretation of God, it is undetermined because God encompasses all things, and the expression of this energy can take on any form, and, no matter what form it takes, it still is a part of God.

Third, any number other than zero divided by zero is meaningless. It is meaningless because any number or a ÷ 0 = b means a = 0 x b. Since 0 x b = 0 for all numbers and (a) can not be zero, the equation is meaningless. Based on our definition of zero, it is meaningless because it is meaningless to think that anything exists other than zero. It is impossible for any number or combination of numbers to not be a part of zero. Since God is as zero, it is meaningless to view ourselves or anything as not being a part of God, because God encompasses all things. There is nothing that can exist separate from God and the idea that there is, is just an illusion.

Now let us examine the relationship that the number one has to all numbers. Other than zero, one is the only number that has meaning in the universe. As we have previously defined, one is zero experiencing itself as love and the essence of all things seen and unseen. There is no such thing as two. It is an illusion. Two is one plus one. There is no such thing as five. Five is one plus one plus one plus one plus one. Five can also be denoted as three plus two. However, three is one plus one plus one and two is one plus one. The numbers three and two are also extensions one. So no matter how the number five is obtained, it breaks down to one plus one plus one plus one plus one. It is still an extension of the number one. If you pull a five-dollar bill out of your wallet, that bill represents five one-dollar bills. You can not say that this thing is five. Five has no meaning without the concept of the number one. Any number greater than one is not separate from one but rather an extension of one. Since God is analogous to zero and one is love, anything or anyone that exists is not separate from God but an extension of God expressed as love.

If all numbers greater than one are just an illusion, there is no number greater than one. Then, the question arises, "Is there a number less than one?" The only whole number less than one is zero. As we stated earlier, zero encompasses all possible numbers, therefore zero is not less than one, one is a part of zero. One is zero experiencing itself as love and the essence of all things. One is love and the experience of love is how we come to know and define for ourselves who God is. So once again God is everything and everything is an expression of God as love.

In summary, nothing can exist that is not a part of God. Not even God can separate itself from God. God never has and never will separate from itself. God can only extend itself through love. Therefore, anything that exists is an extension of God expressed as love.

CHAPTER 0-3

UNDERSTANDING THE TRINITY

To conceive of anything is to have the thought of it.
To create is to make the thought tangible.
To experience is to reflect back to the conceiver
the thought through the creation.

To understand God we must understand the concept of the Trinity. The Trinity in religion is the Father, the Son, and the Holy Spirit. In metaphysics it is Mind, Body and Spirit. These are not two distinct ideas but two different ways of expressing one idea.

The important thing to understand is that the Trinity is not three separate entities but an evolutionary or developmental process of one being. As humans we progress from an infant to a child to an adult. This progression is not the development of three separate individuals but the development of one person. The evolution of God, like the human, is not the evolution of three separate beings but the evolution of one being. The Trinity symbolizes the process through which God creates itself through the experience of itself.

Remember, God is the potential to be anything. Through

God all else exists and is made possible. Another way of stating this is that God is the unlimited potential of creation. When the Bible states that Man was created in the image and likeness of God, it means in her ability to create. It does not mean in her physical image. God has no definable form, even though she can express herself in any form she chooses. The Trinity represents the process of creation or the process through which God experiences itself as God, or more precisely, the process through which God experiences the magnificence of its being and through these experiences expresses its Divinity. To understand God, we need to understand how God creates. We create as God creates; therefore, to understand how God creates, we need to examine how we create.

Since time began, anything created was first conceived as a thought. If the idea of the wheel was never conceived as a thought in someone's mind, it never would have been invented. Therefore, anything created is first conceived as a thought in the mind. Thought is the force behind creation Thought makes creation possible. Thought is pure energy. Thought is the tool of spirit, of God.

The mind is the place where thoughts are collected and processed. Without the mind where would a thought reside? A thought does not originate in the mind. The mind is a depository; like a bank where money is deposited, the mind is where thoughts are deposited. The mind is also the place where thoughts are formalized and become knowable entities. The mind is the instrument through which an idea can be transformed into a tangible experience. Without the mind we would not be able to take an idea such as the wheel and convert it into a tangible object. The mind is the vehicle through which all that exists is created. It is through the mind that God creates everything.

As a next step in the process, after the thought has been received and processed by the mind, the thought can then be acted upon. The thought can be transformed from an idea in the mind to a corporeal experience of the mind. This experience gives the idea its physical life. For example, let us say you get a great idea for a new toy. You must realize that once the mind receives and formulates the idea, it is already a finished product in your mind. All you need to do is transform that thought into a physical object. You need to find a way to take this one-dimensional idea of your toy and make it into a tangible three-dimensional object. You decide to take your idea to a toy-maker and pay them to manufacture your toy. The toy is no longer just an idea in your mind but a tangible object. The toy is a physical experience.

Now let us take a more abstract concept such as kindness. You believe yourself to be a kind person. You know what it means to be kind, but you can not call yourself a kind person until you do an act of kindness. You then decide to help an elderly gentleman carry his groceries home from the store. The thought that you were a kind person is then evidenced in your actions. No longer do you think of yourself as a kind person, you are a kind person.

So the order of creation is conceive-create-experience. Now let us relate this process back to our religious and spiritual trinities. The Holy Spirit is the conceiver, the Father is the creator, and the Son is the experience. The Holy Spirit conceives a thought, the Father creates the idea, and the Son is the tangible embodiment of the Father's creation, thereby reflecting back to the Holy Spirit the idea it had about itself as a physical being. In metaphysical terms the Spirit is the conceiver. The Mind is the creator. The Body is the experience. The Spirit has an idea, the Mind then gives life to the thought, and that creation or idea is experienced through the Body. The circle of creation is complete. An abstract idea is given physical life, and that life is a reflection back to its source, the conceiver of the idea.

If we remember that God is all that exists, the process of creation, symbolized as the Trinity, is the process through which God is experiencing itself through the expression of its Divinity. There is only one Spirit, one Mind and one Body and that is God.

PART II

MEETING OURSELVES

CHAPTER 0 - 4

WHO ARE WE?

W ondrous and
E ternal, we

A rtistically
R ecreate
E nergy

L imitless and
O mnipotent, we
V aliantly
E xperience our divinity

CHAPTER 0 - 5

WHY ARE WE HERE?

To suffer not.
To learn nothing.
To experience everything.
To remember who we are and
choose how we want to express our divinity.

We are not here. We do not exist inside this physical body. Just as Dorothy's body never left her bed while she took her trip to Oz, we never left heaven as we embarked on our journey here on earth. Our existence is outside the body and inside the mind of God, although we can not deny that we seem to be here. Everything seems so real. Ironically, that in our efforts to deny or overcome this physical existence, we give this physical life even more power over us. We need to realize that any reason we give to justify our existence here on earth gives this earthly existence a reality which it does not have and actually keeps us bound to this limited existence. However, there must be some reason for our physical existence, otherwise, why have the experience?

The two most popular schools of thought being taught in our society today are contained within the philosophies of the Christian religion and of Metaphysics. As mentioned earlier, the Christians believe that we are here to try to earn our way back to heaven. We were cast out because we have sinned. Through our pain and our suffering, we can atone for our sin and be allowed to rejoin God in heaven. Metaphysics teaches that we are here to learn. This physical plane is a big schoolroom and everything we experience here is a lesson in our soul's evolution.

We are not here to suffer to atone for any sin. To God, there is no such thing as sin. We do not have to find our way back to heaven because we were never exiled from it. Heaven does not exist as a place. There is nothing we have to do to earn the love of God. It is inherent in who we are. We are not here to struggle. We are here to experience the magnificence of our being. We are not here to be the victim of God's creations. We are here to experience our power as creators.

Neither are we here to learn and evolve our soul. I know that this is the prevailing belief throughout the spiritual movement today, and the difference between the point I am making here and this belief may only be one of semantics, but I think it is a point which needs some clarification. It is O.K. to think of this as a learning experience as long as that learning has nothing to do with the concept of right and wrong or good and evil, and everything to do with helping you to decide who you want to be and how you want to represent your Godhead. Remember, in God there is no polarity. There is no such thing as right and wrong or good and evil; those concepts are illusions. Also, we are not here to evolve the soul. The soul exists as it always exists, as pure unlimited potential. It is impossible to evolve beyond this point. It is O.K. to think of everything as evolving as long as evolution is **not** viewed as a movement upwards from a lower state to a higher state, but as a transition or unfolding from one state to another. The universal concept of evolution is comparable to that of a caterpillar before it transforms itself into a butterfly. The caterpillar contains within it all the same genes that it carries as a butterfly. The caterpillar is not evolving into a butterfly—it **is** the butterfly before it transforms from one state to another.

We are not here to learn how to love. Love can not be learned in a classroom. It is not contained in any book. Love can only be expressed. We are here to express the love that we are.

We are not here to learn how to create. We are creators. All we do is create. We are creating every second of every minute of every day.

We are not here to learn that we are spiritual beings. As Ram Dass so aptly put it, "We are spiritual beings having a physical experience." This physical existence is not the reality of who we are.

Experience. Experience. Experience. We are here to experience. When something is done for the experience of it, it is not done as an act of repentance. It is not done to learn something. It is something we do just for the joy of doing it. So when someone asks, "Why did you climb that mountain?" tell them, "Because it was there." We do not have to justify anything. No other reason need be given. The only thing we need to do is to remember we are not life's victim, we are its creator. We need only to decide what we want to express about ourselves through the experience. The experience is an expression of who we are; it does not define who we are. Our experiences reflect back to us our thoughts about ourselves. Since we are love, or the vehicle through which God expresses its Divinity, we reflect back to God all the thoughts it has about itself. It is through this physical experience that God will experience the magnificence of its being.

We have nothing to learn or to atone for, but we have everything to experience. We are here as a way for God, our creator to experience its Divinity. We are here to remember we are expressions of God and to express the love that we are. We are here to create experiences, to have an adventure, to have fun, and experience all the glory that this life has to offer us. We are here to experience the magnificence of our being, and through our experiences we ultimately choose how we will represent God in the universe.

CHAPTER 0-6

UNCOVERING THE ILLUSION

*If what we think of as illusion is, in truth, real and
if what we think of as real is, in truth, illusion, then
what we thought to be the illusion becomes our reality and
what we thought to be real becomes our illusion.*

In this text, God is represented by the number zero and humanity is represented by the number one. The only question that has not yet been answered completely is, "How did God get from O to 1?" How did God create Man? Did God implode and divide itself into billions of pieces and through a process of evolution create the universe and all life within it, as proposed in the Big Bang Theory? Or, did God create Man and the universe in six days out of dust as taught in the Christian religion? The answer to this question has been hinted at all throughout the text but never directly stated. God made us up. He imagined us. We exist as thought in the mind of God.

I bring up this point not to try to propose a new theory as to how we got here, but to make the point that we are not here at all. Both theories suggest that everything was created separately, either through division of God into billions of pieces or as separate thought projections outside the mind of God. Both theories suggest a reality separate from God, and my point is that there is no reality separate from

God, and any explanation just supports an illusion. We were never created. We still exist as we always existed, as energy, as spirit. The universal concept of creation has nothing to do with physical creation but involves only Spirit/God as an extension of itself. God creates as we create. God creates through thought, which is an extension of itself. Just as our thoughts are a part of us, we, as God's thoughts, are a part of God. God can not create anything separate from Self because nothing else exists.

Thought is the tool of spirit. Creation can only take place in the realm of spirit. It is in the mind, which is the instrument of spirit, that thought is stored and processed.[4] The universe is a thought creation and everything in it is an extension of spirit. There is only one spirit and one mind, the spirit and mind of God, and all thought takes place within the mind of God. Spirit is all that is real. Anything that is not spirit or anything that exists within space and time is an illusion. So anything material or physical is **not** real.

Just as we create mirrors as a way to see ourselves and those mirrors are illusory reflections of ourselves which enable us to see ourselves from a vantage point outside of ourselves, so this physical plane was created by God as a reflection of Self back to Self. Through this physical experience, God could experience Self from a vantage point

---

[4] The mind should not be confused with the brain. The mind, like spirit and thought, exists in a realm beyond space and time, a place where time and space do not exist. The brain is an instrument of the body and is **not** where the mind resides.

outside of Self, but since such a vantage point does not exist, such a vantage point has to be created as an illusion, as a dream. Man or the body, depending on our religious or spiritual affiliation, is an illusory experience or reflection of thought back to Self. In the same way that our dreams are illusions of the mind, this physical existence is an illusion or dream within the mind of God, because our mind is God's mind.

God never divided itself. God never created us a separate entity. There never was any explosion. We were never formed out of dust. We are God. We are both the creator and the created, and this existence is no more than a fairy tale or adventure story in our mind. This life is no more than an elaborate dream, a dream through which we experience our divinity and we evolve our spirit.

I know this is hard to believe, but if an illusionist such as David Copperfield can have us believe that he can make the Statue of Liberty vanish before our eyes, do you believe that we, as God, do not have the power to make ourselves believe that this life is real? We as God are the greatest illusionist of all time, and this is an illusion we are creating for ourselves. Imagine that you are sitting in the audience of a master ventriloquist. He and his dummy are having a conversation with the audience. The ventriloquist never forgets the dummy is not real; however, after a few minutes you are drawn into the illusion. You believe the dummy is alive. You then have to remind yourself that the dummy is made of wood. The same thing has happened here, but we just have not yet re-minded ourselves that this is a dream.

We have not yet decided to re-join the mind of God to awaken ourselves from the illusion of our existence. This is why the process of enlightenment or self-actualization is called Remembrance. When we re-member, we decide to once again be a member of the whole. We choose to be a part of the whole, not separate from the whole. We choose to no longer live a life in the illusion of separation from God, but we decide to live our life as part of God, which is who we are.

It is important to remember that God does not exist here because we do not exist here. God is not even aware that a separation exists and never has or never will leave its unified state. Let us, for a moment, pretend our consciousness is confined in the head of our physical body. As we look out over our body we see our feet, our legs, our hands, etc. Now we begin to focus our attention on our right-hand index finger and wonder to ourselves what it is like to be that finger? We then project our consciousness into that finger and begin to look back at our body. We then stretch our arm way out so we can get a good look at our entire body. We see **a** foot, **a** leg, **a** hand, etc. Now as we do this, the mind knows that the finger suspended in air surveying the body is a part of the body. The mind knows that it is the whole body and the finger simultaneously and that the finger has not left the wholeness of the body. However, the finger looking back at the whole body experiences space between itself and the rest of the body and feels separate from the body, even though the separation it feels is an illusion. Just as the consciousness of the whole body will always see itself from its vantage point as being whole, God is unaware of any separation among its parts and exists as it always exists, whole and unified. However, just like the finger looking back at the whole body, we feel separate from the whole, but this separation is an illusion. We are God, and as God looking upon itself we are one unified consciousness. However, as a thought in the mind of God looking back at the whole mind, we feel separated from the whole mind; but this separation, we must remember, is not real.

I make this last point so we can realize that a separate God does not exist and that a separate God does not create the world we live in. We are God, and we create our own life, and collectively we create the world we live in. If we are waiting for some entity separate from ourselves to come down and save us and solve all our problems, we will be waiting forever. Everyone and everything is God, or there is no God, these are the choices. Just as our thoughts are not separate from us, we are not separate from God. Until we can accept that we are expressions of God, we will never know God, and God will never know itself experientially. It would be as if we had a dream of one day vacationing on a tropical beach, all the time knowing it is a dream; then one day we find ourselves walking out onto that beach. The dream is no longer a dream; it is a real experience. Well, God dreamed of one day knowing itself experientially, and this is the illusion that was created to accomplish this task. Through this dream God will experience the magnificence of its being, and we will come to know that we are God.

Until the day we can awaken to the fact that we are God and be that God, God will never experience what it is to be God. God will never know what it is like to walk out onto that beach.

Exercise: Each morning, once during the day, and at night before going to bed remind yourself that you are dreaming. Remind yourself that your physical body and this limited physical existence are not the reality of who you are.

PART III

UNDERSTANDING THE
PARADOX

CHAPTER 0-7

DEFINING REMEMBRANCE

To know God is to know ourselves.
To know ourselves is to know God.
The only way to know God is to remember we are God.

Enlightenment. Self-Actualization. Atonement. Salvation. These are all synonyms for the process of Remembrance. It is the process through which we move from feeling separate from God to being at one with God. It is the process through which we give up our individual self for our Divine Self. It is the process through which we choose to live our life through love and not fear. To relate this to our mathematical terms, God is zero and God is everything. God expressed is one and is all that exists. If you add one to any number it enlarges that number or increases its separation from zero. However, when one is subtracted from any number, it decreases that number and lessens its separation from zero. If one is continually subtracted from a number, the number eventually returns to one. And if you subtract one from itself, it returns to zero. Remembrance is our returning to zero. It is the step-by-step return from seeing everyone and everything as separate from ourselves to seeing everyone and everything as a part of us. Then, taking the final step of subtracting out our individual self, we return to our Divine Self—seeing ourselves and everything as a part of God. This is what Jesus meant when he said in the Bible "My father and I are one." This is Christ Consciousness.

The first thing we need to understand is that this journey is definitely a process. It is not something that happens in the blink of an eye or in a flash of light. We do not suddenly awaken one day and see the light and vanish into thin air. When we become enlightened, we do not become a non-entity. It is exactly the opposite. We expand the idea of who we are to include everyone and everything. We no longer exist as an individual. We exist as a part of the whole and the whole is God. Through this process a life lived in fear is transformed into a life lived through love.

Enlightenment is a movement from free will to freedom. We give up our free will or the view that life is a choice between two separate forces—the forces of love and fear or good and evil. Instead, we choose to live a life of freedom where we have only one choice, and that is the choice for love. To the enlightened soul, love is all that exists, and everything is as an expression of love.

We also need to understand that through this process we are not trying to become perfect beings. We already are perfect beings. We are not here to change the circumstances of our lives but to realize that our lives are already perfect. Life continues on as before. The only aspect that changes is our attitude towards our lives. Our lives no longer define us, they express who we are. We understand that there is no such thing as imperfection. It is no accident the word

perfection is contained within the word im**perfection**. There is perfection in everything, even in what we consider imperfect. Imperfection is the illusion. Perfection is all that exists.

The goal of this process is not to make the earth vanish but to have us awaken within the dream. There is a technique being taught around the country called "Lucid Dreaming." It teaches people how to be conscious participants in their dreams. The person is trained how to wake up inside their dreams and to take an active role in recreating their dreams. Now all we have to do is transfer this same process to our so-called waking state: to know that this world we think we live in is also a dream, and that the separation we feel from God is as much an illusion.

The most important thing to remember about this process is that this self-realization, this awakening, is not something that just happens to us, but it is something **we choose**. We must choose to awaken from this dream.

Why do we forget things? Why do we not remember a person's name or the name of a restaurant? Why can't we call forth the thought whenever we want or need it? The reason is that the mind is not in control of the thought. If the mind had the control, the thought would never be forgotten. The thought is the decision-maker in the process. It is the thought that must decide to rejoin the mind. Then and only then is the thought remembered. Remember, we were created as thought—a thought in the mind of God. We are the thought in this scenario. We have the control. It is not

God's decision to awaken us to a remembrance of who we are. It is ours. We must choose to remember we are an expression of God.

The way to remember we are an expression of God is to remind ourselves that we are an expression of God. We have to consciously decide to rejoin the infinite mind of God. We re-mind ourselves with the mind of God and re-member we are an expression of God the same way we re-mind ourselves of anything else. We memorize it. We have to keep repeating it over and over until we do not forget. When we remind ourselves that we are an expression of God we rejoin the mind of God. We heal the separation we feel from God and all of life. We become one with God; we have **at-one-ment**.

Exercise: Each day when you awake, once during the day and before you retire for the night say aloud three times "I AM GOD and I AM CHRIST." These words should be stated out loud, with conviction, and as truth. Do not keep these words trapped in your mind or whisper them under your breath. Words and ideas said aloud carry even greater power than thought. These words are extremely powerful and through this exercise you are expressing that you and everything that exists is an individualized expression of God, all of which are spiritually equal, with no one expression being any greater or more loved than any other. These spoken words will lead you to a greater experience of yourself and your divinity.

CHAPTER 0 - 8

THE RELATIVE UNIVERSE

What is good without the concept of evil?
What is love without the concept of fear?
What is God without the concept of Man?
What is can only be defined by that which it is not.

If God is everything and all that exists then what does it mean to be God? That is an impossible question to answer. God is an abstraction even to itself. God is "nothing." What is black if everything that exists is black? God is unlimited, all-powerful, loving, and creative but had no way to experience that knowledge. As previously stated, to believe yourself to be a kind person is only a concept in your mind until it is evidenced by a kind act. Then you have become a kind person. God desired to know itself as more than just a concept. He wanted to experience all of his magnificence. It is with this desire that God extended itself as both the metaphysical and physical universe. When God created itself as the physical universe, he created himself as the laws that govern this physical plane of existence, not the earth itself. When God created itself as the metaphysical universe, he created himself as spirit, in the image and likeness of itself, with a unity consciousness, and as creator. It is with this power as creators that we create our bodies, our lives, and this earth. In creating itself as the metaphysical and physical universe, God created a way to know itself experientially. In the instant these two universes were created, the illusion that there exists a reality separate from God was created as a reference point through which God could experience itself.

To further clarify this point, if God is A and all that exists, then in order for God to know itself experientially, it would have to create a contrasting reference point or a B. However, at the same time he created B, he would have to create the space between A and the B, so they could exist as separate entities. So, A is God, B is the physical universe or matter, and the space separating A and B is the metaphysical universe or spirit.

To understand the relationship A has to B, we need to refer back to our mathematical analogy. God is zero. Zero is eternal and unlimited. In order to understand itself as unlimited and eternal God needed a contrasting reference point as a comparison, so God created one. One is God expressing itself as love or Man in physical form. Man is finite and limited. Even though one can not exist without zero, zero has no meaning without the concept of one. In the absence of that which it is not, that which is trying to be defined has no meaning. God reasoned that the only way it could understand and experience itself as eternal and unlimited is through the experience of its opposite or by experiencing itself as limited and finite. This is the concept of relativity.

What does it mean to be kind if you do not know what it is to be unkind? It is through the experience of the unkind act that we define the kind act. Without the other, each concept is unknowable. Without God, Man can not exist, and without Man, God is unknown to itself. This relationship, the defining of what something is by that which it is not, is the premise on which this entire universe is designed. This is the theory behind our relative universe: a universe in which everything is defined relative to what it is not.

Probably the most difficult aspect of the universe to understand is that there are three universes occurring at the same time. This is why physicality is called the Third Dimension. Since nothing can exist that is not God, God, which is neither the metaphysical or the physical, is also expressed as both. The metaphysical universe or the thought God has of itself, expressed as love; the physical universe or the thought God has of itself that it is not, expressed as fear; and God as it is or the unlimited potential of creation, exist simultaneously as three aspects of one God. These are not three separate forces but three different expressions of the same force. So, God is neither male or female but is expressed as both male and female. God is neither good or evil but at the same time is evidenced by that which we consider good and that which we consider evil. Good and evil, health and illness, joy and sadness are not separate forces but different ways of experiencing one force, all of which is God.

46   AWAKENING FROM OZ

In order for God to know itself experientially as Creator, God had to un-create itself as Man. Man and the physical universe would be the vehicle through which God could experience itself. Through physicality Man would recreate itself as God, and through this process God would have the experience of itself. This is the knowledge Adam and Eve obtained when they bit the apple. God did not throw them out of the Garden, they chose to leave. Leaving the Garden, or more accurately, forgetting their connection with God was the only way that they could come to know themselves as God. We left heaven and entered hell in order to understand the experience of heaven. We had to perceive ourselves as separate physical beings before we could know ourselves as one spiritual force.

We need to understand that without fear there is no choice. Fear is not bad. Fear is not good. Fear is an illusion. However, without the illusion of fear, we would have no way of understanding our true nature. Just as without the experience of sadness, we would not know joy, or without the experience of evil, we would not know what is good, through our experiences with fear we are able to come to know ourselves as love. It is because of our experiences with fear that we are able to reconnect with our Godself through the experience of joy.

The beliefs we hold about ourselves and the universe we live in are completely opposite of the truth. This was done by design. In the absolute where our creator exists there is no polarity. There is no up or down, good or bad, right or wrong. However, polarity is the only way to experience absoluteness. It was a blessing for us to believe that we left the Garden of Eden, not a failing. We needed to believe ourselves as separate from God, our creator. It was necessary that we experience fear so we could know love. Without a relative universe, God could never experience itself as God. Without a relative universe, there would be no choice. We would have no way of defining ourselves and recreating ourselves as God. It is through our relationship to God that God experiences itself, and it is through our relationship with other people and this physical universe that we define who we are and who we want to be.

As Man, we already have the experience of God, but we have shielded ourselves from the knowledge that we are God. God, our creator, knows it is God but desires to know itself experientially. Through this relative universe our creator is on a journey to experiencing itself, and we, his creations, are on a journey to remembering we are God. Through our experiences we are being presented choices and through our choices we are recreating ourselves as God. We are deciding how we want to represent ourselves as God in the universe. Not until we remember that we are expressions of God will God exist as a knowable entity and experience the overwhelming magnificence of its being.

CHAPTER 0 - 9

UNIVERSAL PRINCIPLES

What we sow, so shall we reap.
What we give, so shall we receive.
What we think, so shall we be.

The universe is very simple in design. All life began as thought. Thought is pure energy, and this is how we create our lives. We make our lives much more difficult than necessary because we lack knowledge and understanding of the basic elements of the law which governs this level of consciousness. Even though we create our lives, the process through which we create is not our creation; it is **not** who we are. We are spirit and as spirit we use these laws to create our bodies, our lives, and this earth. It is not necessary that we understand all the physical laws of this universe any more than we, as a driver of a car, would need to know all the mechanics of how the engine works before we could drive the car. The only law we need to know and understand is the law which governs creation itself.

As I stated earlier, we were created as extensions of God in the image and likeness of itself as creator. We create as God creates. God creates through thought. We as God have the power to create through thought. Also as God, we have the ability to create whatever we choose. We have the free will to create all the circumstances of our lives. We have before us each second of every day unlimited possibilities from which to create our lives. Whatever we focus our attention on is what will be made manifest in our lives. Our lives are physical representations of our thoughts and beliefs about ourselves and the world we live in. Our lives represent the natural playing out of the laws which govern this plane of existence. Therefore, in order for us to create the life we want, we need to know and understand the founding principles of this universe.

The universal law which rules creation in this dimension of existence is the "Law of Cause and Effect," sometimes referred to as the "Law of Karma" or the "Law of Giving and Receiving." This law outlines the circular flow of energy which radiates throughout the universe. To put it simply, every action has a reaction, and that reaction reflects the action. Or every cause has an effect, and the effect is a reflection of the cause. Therefore, in order for us to receive love (the effect or reaction), we need to give love (the cause or the action). We cannot receive love without first giving love. Whatever we give is what we receive. So whatever experience we desire in our lives must first be extended out into the universe before it can be returned to us. To be happy we must share our happiness. To feel secure we must give security to others. We as the cause will also be our own effect. In sharing our happiness with others, that feeling of happiness is returned to us and increases our own feeling of happiness. In giving security to others our own sense of security is strengthened within us.

Before we continue I would like to clear up some confusion that exists around our understanding of the concept of karma. Karma is **not** some cosmic debt or punishment for the sins of our past. We do not suffer in this life as a form of repayment or punishment for actions in our past lives. Karma represents the sum total of all our experiences or the person we are today, and it is from this perspective that our soul draws to decide which experiences to create that would best serve us in bringing us closer to the true nature of our existence. It is through the law of karma that we are able to see who we are now, and from this reference point we decide if this is who we want to be and if the life we are living best represents the person we want to be.

One of the problems we encounter in the application of this law is that we forget that the universe is non-judgmental and impartial and gives us exactly what we ask for. This law is constantly at work helping us create exactly what we choose each moment of every day. A challenge arises when we do not understand how the universe interprets our thoughts. The universe interprets our thoughts **literally**, and, through the law of cause and effect, makes them our reality. If we wish we had a new job, the verb or the action the universe acts on is the wish. The wishing for the new job is what we get, not the new job. If we want a new house, the action the universe acts on is the want. The wanting for the new house is what we receive, not the new house. If we need a new car, the action the universe returns to us is the need. The needing of the new car is what we get, not the new car. The only way to make manifest in our lives what we desire is to have it. And the only way to have something before experiencing it physically is to conceive of it mentally or with what is known religiously as faith. Faith is knowing something is given before it is experienced as a physical reality. Remember, the order of creation is conceive-create-experience. We must have the thought of it first before it can be created and then experienced. We must believe we have the new car before it can be created and manifested in our lives. So if we can not conceive ourselves as having it, it will never be manifested in our lives.

The type of faith we need is the faith that allows us to be thankful in advance for something that has not yet been manifested in our reality, to know that whatever we desire is on its way to us now. The problem is that we cannot lie. We cannot trick the universe into giving us something we do not believe we already have. The intent behind the thanksgiving must be in alignment with our beliefs. We will not experience abundance in our lives if we do not feel the abundance. We will not experience abundance in our lives if all we dwell on is what we lack. We will not experience the unlimited abundance of the universe if we believe that it does not exist. We will not experience the unlimited abundance of the universe if we do not feel we are worthy of such abundance. Remember, what we focus on is what we receive. If the focus of our lives is on what we lack, lack is what we receive.

The fact of the matter is not that we do not have abundance in our lives, but that we do not have as much abundance as we want. In order for us to receive more abundance, we have to first be **truly thankful** for the abundance that we already have in our lives. This will open the door for more abundance to flow into our lives. For example, if we **want** the love of a companion and all we think about is how we **lack** that love, we will receive exactly what we are focusing on. We will get the wanting for that love because we are focusing on the lack of love. Instead, what we should be doing is focusing on all the love that we already have in our lives: the love of our families, our friends, our pets, or any other source of love in our lives. This will open the door for more love to flow into our lives. The universe does not distinguish between different types of love. The soul is after a feeling experience, which takes form as our physical reality. The soul does not concern itself with the circumstances we create to achieve that feeling.

However, even if we focus on all that we have so that we open the flow for more of it to come into our lives, this does not guarantee that it will be manifested. Our thoughts are multi-layered. Our conscious beliefs about ourselves and our lives are built upon deeper, more formative beliefs we hold as truths about ourselves and the world we live in. These core beliefs are the foundation from which our entire life experience is manifested. These are the controlling beliefs in our lives. For example, let us say you have a strong conscious desire to be a good person. Being a good person gives purpose to your life. As a child you were taught and accepted the belief that money is bad and is the root of all evil. Also, through your religious training you came to believe that suffering is the way to heaven. Denial and poverty in this physical life will be rewarded in heaven. Only good people go to heaven. As an adult these beliefs will not be consciously remembered in your everyday thoughts. You now desire wealth and abundance. You work hard, but it never seems to get you anywhere. You even concentrate on creating more abundance, but it never seems to materialize. The reason is that your desire to be a good person is stronger, more deeply rooted than your desire to be wealthy. Everything you associate with being good means to suffer and be impoverished. Money and abundance are evil, and you do not want to be evil. Your desire to be good will override any attempt at obtaining your wealth. To create the abundance you desire, you must first change your core beliefs surrounding wealth and abundance.

In order for us to change any area of our lives, we must first uncover those foundation beliefs we hold as our truths. The only way we can uncover our core beliefs is to take a look at what is being manifested in our lives. Our lives are telling us everything we believe about ourselves and the world we live in. The goal is not to try to change all our core beliefs, just the ones that do not work in our lives. The beliefs that do not represent the person we want to be.

One of the greatest misconceptions we have about this universe is the belief that there are levels or gradations. We as humans try to make everything right or wrong, good or bad, loving or fearful when in fact they are the same. In our lives we place value judgments on everything, judgments that often lead to our taking contradictory positions. In our minds it is more blessed to give than receive. It is more sacred to be a nun, a social worker or Peace Corps volunteer than a plumber or electrician. And yet we value the C.E.O. of a company or a doctor more than the factory worker or flight attendant because they make more money. It is wrong to steal a million dollars from a bank, but it is acceptable steal a quarter from our relatives or a pen from work. We say it is wrong to murder, and yet we murder as a form of punishment. We value human life more than animal life and animal life more than plant life. We criticize people for killing animal meat for food, when we kill animals for clothing and plant life for food. The universe does not recognize any of these so-called values that we place on people, places, things, or events in our lives. All jobs are the same. Stealing is stealing. Killing is killing. The same life force that animates human life animates all life. To the universe they are all the same. Every person, every place, every event, every thing is God expressing itself as love.

God, the universe, is not rewarding or punishing us based on what we do. God, the universe, is not teaching us lessons. God, the universe, is giving us everything we choose based on our thoughts. Our life is our creation based on our beliefs about ourselves and the world we live in. Life was a gift from our creator. What we do with it and how we choose to live it is our choice.

Exercise: Have a talk with yourself. First decide the areas of your life you desire to change. Then write down all your beliefs surrounding those topics. Write everything down that pops into your head. Everything your parents told you. Everything your clergy told you. Everything you learned in school. Everything you learned from friends. Any cliché phrases that come to mind. You never know for sure what you may have unknowingly adopted as your truth. After the list is compiled, examine each phrase and observe if it is operating in your life.

PART IV

THE PATH
TO ENLIGHTENMENT

CHAPTER 0 - 10

THE ROAD TO MASTERY

""The true master is the one who knows
that the only thing to master in life
is mastering itself."

One of the first steps after accepting that we create our lives is to understand that everything from which we create our lives is learned. What we call our truths are no more than acquired knowledge based on ideas that may not be true. We create our reality from choices offered by others, and it is from these choices that we decide what to believe about ourselves, God, and the world we live in. Even the feelings we attach to the events in our lives are a learned behavior. We accept as truth that it is correct to feel sad when someone dies or to feel happy at the birth of a new baby. We are taught what is right and what is wrong. We are taught what is good and what is evil. However, we fail to comprehend that the event itself is neutral. **We** label the event. **We** choose how we want to feel. **We** have the power to decide how we are going to react to every event or experience in our lives. The event has no power of its own. We are the ones, we give away our power to the experience and allow the experience to define and control us.

Once we accept the fact that everything is learned and we have the power to change it, then we no longer have to be a victim in life. No longer do we have to blame others for the circumstances of our lives. We realize there is no reason to complain, only to change. We understand that to change the reality of our lives, we need to change **our** beliefs and thoughts about it. We must examine our beliefs, because everything we experience is designed to support those beliefs. We understand that we cannot change our beliefs by changing our outward experience. The experience is the result of the belief, not the other way around. We do not formulate our beliefs based on what we experience. The belief comes first and then we create the experience as a projection of the belief. I am not suggesting that we need to discard everything that we hold as truth, but we need to start questioning everything that we have been taught to believe about ourselves, God, and the world we live in. We need to examine what beliefs are keeping us from living the life we desire. We need to examine what beliefs are preventing us from being the person we want to be. Just because our parents may have taught us that money is scarce, that it doesn't grow on trees, or the church has taught us that God is to be feared, this does not mean that it has to be our truth. We need to understand what it means to be an adult. We need to start **thinking for ourselves** and **making our own decisions**. We start by examining all our thoughts, all our beliefs and decide if they represent the type of life we want to have and the person we want to be. We must then decide which thoughts and beliefs we choose to keep and which thoughts and beliefs we choose to discard. We need to accept the power we have as creators. We need to reclaim our lives as our creations. In this acceptance we take full responsibility for everything that happens in life. It is in the reclaiming of our power and the retraining of our minds that we can begin to create the life we desire and become the person we choose to be.

Exercise: Start off by setting aside 10 minutes three times a day for mental examinations. Sitting upright in a comfortable chair, pick an area of your life you desire to change. Start examining all your thoughts surrounding that subject. After each completed thought, decide if the thought is still a valuable thought you wish to keep or a belief you wish to change. Decide if this is the type of thought that represents the life you want and the person you want to be. If you decide it is a thought you wish to keep, then nothing need be done, but if it is a thought you wish to change, then you need to cancel the thought. To cancel a thought you say after the thought, "I cancel that thought" and then you affirm the opposite. For example, let us say you believe that you will never have the abundance in life you desire. Any time any thought comes to mind to support that belief say, "I cancel that thought," and then say, "The universe is a place of unlimited abundance, and it is on its way to me now." Or say anything that feels comfortable and represents how you want your life to be. Then start focusing on all the abundance you already have in your life.

The more you do this, the easier it becomes. Before you

know it, you will be canceling out negative thoughts and replacing them with new positive thoughts all throughout the day. Remember, you have to conceive the new thought first before it can be experienced as your reality.

This leads us into another step in the process of mastering life, and that is the realization that everything in life is a choice. We are willing participants in all the events of our lives. There is nothing in what we do or nothing in the way we act that is not our choice. We need to realize that, even if we clean the garage after three grueling months of constant nagging from our spouse, that we are doing it because at that point we choose to do it. We are not doing it as a result of their nagging, because we could choose to let them continue to nag us. It is even our choice to get angry when someone cuts us off in traffic. Not everyone gets angry so, why do we?

We create the events in our lives to produce experiences which evoke the feeling of love or fear. Love is any emotion which expands, shares, strengthens, heals, or unites us with others, such as joy, happiness, compassion, and contentment. Fear is any emotion which confines, restricts, limits, weakens, decreases, or separates us from others, such as sorrow, anger, hatred, envy, and self-pity. Love or fear, these are the only two choices we have for experiencing the events in our lives, however we decide which of these feelings to experience. Free will is not only the ability to create all the events in our lives, but also the ability to choose if the event will be an experience of love or an experience of fear. Everything in life revolves around this choice. Remember, without the experience of fear, we could not know and experience love. Without the experience of fear, we would not be able to choose love and experience our true nature. Without love we could not recreate our divinity. Without love we could not experience ourselves as God. However, we can never forget that love is our true nature. Love is all that exists. Fear is an illusion.

Exercise: Each time you encounter a situation that you label as fearful, do not ask yourself, "What is it that I fear?" but tell yourself "I am experiencing love," then ask yourself "How do I choose to represent myself in the face of this experience?"

The more you uncover fear as the illusion it is, the less it has to be a part of your life. The more you acknowledge love, the more love becomes a part of your life. Continue to do this, and there will come a time when love will be the only experience you have in your life.

One of the most difficult steps to master in life is to make the choice for non-attachment, or the ability to act without any attachment to a specific result(s). We do everything in life because we expect something in return. We give so we can receive. We work so we can get paid. We love so we can be loved. If we do not think we are getting something in return or what we think we deserve, we see no reason to do it in the first place. Our greatest suffering comes from the expectations we place on ourselves, God, and the other people in our lives. In conjunction with every thought and action is a feeling. (Feelings are also the tool of spirit.) We do what we do not just for what it can bring us physically or materially but for what feeling we think it will produce. We would be happy if__(fill in the blank). However, we must remember that the feeling we associate with a thought or experience is a learned response. All events are neutral by nature—if they were not then every person would react identically to every experience. For instance, if money made a person happy, then all rich people would be happy, which clearly is not the case. We choose to react to each and every experience in our lives by feeling bad or good. We decide to experience the event as loving or fearful. Once we detach from the experience, we can step back and choose how we view each experience and decide how we want to represent ourselves in relationship to the experience. The event or experience no longer controls us. We no longer react but choose to act. Our actions become consciously motivated. We act the way we do because it is our decision to act that way, not because we have no choice. We evolve to the point where the act itself is the reason for the action, not what we expect in return. If we do something because we expect something in return either physically or emotionally, we are leaving ourselves open for pain and disappointment. However, if the act itself is its own reward and we choose the feeling we want to experience and then experience it, it does not matter what if anything we get in return.

Exercise: Each time you decide to do something, ask yourself if the act itself is enough to produce what you want regardless of what you may receive. Decide how you want to experience the event and have the experience before the event is enacted. For example, do not take your mother to the store because it will make you feel good. First feel good about taking your mother to the store, and then take her to the store. The decision to feel good before the experience will create a joyful experience. And, even if your mother is not appreciative of your taking her to the store, it will not matter.

Once we accept that we create our lives and that we also choose how we will react to the experiences of our lives, it also becomes easier to not judge the experience or the participant(s) in the experience. We cannot forget that we create these experiences to give us choices of how to re-create our divinity. At the same time that we are using the experience to define ourselves, likewise the other participants are using the experience to define themselves. Our job is to decide how we want to define ourselves in relationship to the experience and not to label or judge how the other participants are using the same experience. We define ourselves and our lives through each experience and how we interpret that experience. I am not saying that we should not define something as right or wrong or good or evil, but that we **cannot** define other peoples' lives by the way we interpret our experiences. In the absolute there is no right or wrong. There is no good or evil. We define that for ourselves. What we need to do is to accept our truths as **our truths** and allow others their truths. Allow the other person to make their choices. It is in trying to convince others that our way is the correct way that we experience pain.

Exercise: Every time you encounter a situation that you want to judge as either right or wrong or good or evil, ask yourself these questions; "Why cannot both options be correct?" "Why is my way correct?" "Why is my way the only way?" Then **bless**, don't judge the other person(s) for presenting you that choice, and decide which position best represents the person you want to be. And always remember to allow the other person(s) their choice.

One of the most beneficial steps on the road to mastering life is learning to live within the paradox of life. We need to understand that we are living in a reverse reality—that everything we believe is completely opposite of the truth. We believe that we are physical beings, when the reality is that we are spiritual beings. We believe that our mind is localized within the brain of this physical body, when its existence is outside the boundaries of time and space. We believe that we have no control in our lives, when actually our lives are our creations. We believe God is a separate entity from ourselves, when the truth is we are expressions of God. At the same time, we need to realize and understand the importance of this physical experience. It was necessary for us to experience the opposite of our true nature in order for us to understand and experience what our true nature is. We needed to believe ourselves as physical beings before we could understand ourselves as spiritual beings.

In learning to live within this paradox, we must unlearn all that we have learned, so we can recreate ourselves into the person we want to be. To unlearn all that we have learned, we must face each situation in our lives as if we are a blank sheet of paper. We must erase all our expectations, our preconceived ideas of who we are and what we have been taught to believe. We must stop thinking with our minds and start thinking with our hearts by paying attention to how we feel. We need to stop trying to define who we are by what we do. Instead, we must first decide who we want to be and let our lives be a reflection of that person. It is in being the person we want to be that we become that person; we cannot become anything that we are not already.

Our lives are always a reflection of who we are and what we believe, even if we do not consciously realize it. Do not search to find what you think you are missing in people, places, and things outside yourself. Do not seek happiness in wealth, power, or fame. These things can not bring you happiness. Be happy with yourself and your life as it is now. Then wealth, power, and fame can be an expression of your happiness, but your happiness will not depend on it. In the past, we would give love or what we thought was love, in the hopes of getting love in return. However, living within the paradox, we understand that we can not give anything to another that we do not have ourselves. If we do not love ourselves, we have no love to give to another. If we do not feel secure ourselves, we can not help others to feel secure. We will not find happiness in the happiness of others if we are not happy ourselves. In extending our own happiness to others, we make others happy. Even though it is easier for many of us to give than to receive, if you are unable to receive, eventually you will have nothing to give. We have to come to a point in our evolution where we realize the importance of being Self-centered. However, being Self-centered without first accepting that you are an expression of God will only bind you more to this physical existence and increase the separation you feel from God. True Self-centeredness is being centered in God, in your divinity.

Being Self-centered does not mean that we do nothing for other people, but that we do it because it is an expression of who we want to be. It is our joy. There is nothing we should or should not do other than express the person we want to be and do whatever it is that releases the joy we feel. Remember, the soul is after a feeling experience, not a physical one. The particular circumstances of our lives do not matter to the soul. The soul expresses itself through feelings of joy, so whatever makes us feel joyful is the way we connect to our soul and the way we express and experience our divinity. As we progress along this path and stop denying our joy, we come to realize that our joy is reflected in others as their joy, and the joy of others is reflected in us as our joy. Our joy is their joy and their joy is our joy. Joy unites us as one being.

Exercise: Each time before you act ask yourself, "How does this make me feel?" If it does not make you feel good and reflect the person you want to be, then do not do it.

Now is the time to take responsibility and accept that we create everything in our lives. Also, recognize that we choose how we view each experience and how we will react to the experience. No longer be a victim in life nor blame or judge others. We have the God-given power to change the circumstances we no longer desire. It is ours and always has been.

Reclaim your power. Recreate your life. Let your life reflect the person you choose to be. There is no greater joy.

CHAPTER 0-11

RETURNING TO ONE

When we look in the mirror
we are looking at the face of love.
When we look into the face of another
we are looking at ourselves.

As we progress along this path, we come to the point where we begin to gain greater clarity and understanding. We seek truth at the highest level, and that truth is revealed to us as oneness. There is only one force in the universe and that is love. We are the expression of that love force in physical form. We as a whole—every person, every act—is a reflection of that love force in action. There is nothing in life that is not a part of that love. All of life is a mirror, and everyone and every event in our lives is a playing out of our inner reality. Everyone and everything that exists, exists inside of us, as a part of our self. The person who is screaming at us for making a mistake is our self. The person who is abusing us is our self. The person we are abusing is our self. When we judge another person, the person we are judging is our self.

People are in our lives to reflect back to us what is inside us so we can choose if this is how we want to represent our Godhead. We are shown the many facets of our divinity, and we then choose from all that we are shown to define who we are and how we want to represent our unique expression of God as love in the universe.

If we are to find the joy, peace, happiness, and love we seek, we must stop denying who we are. We must to stop denying the various aspects of our being. We do not encounter prejudice in our lives because people are prejudiced. The prejudiced people are in our lives to show us that we are prejudiced. If it was not within us, we would not be able to recognize it in another. We need to face all the skeletons in our closet, or they will never go away. What we resist persists. What we accept we can change. We must face all our fears. We need to own up to all that we consider good and bad about ourselves. By avoiding or denying any part of ourselves that we think is bad or evil, we give that bad or evil part of ourselves a seemingly real existence: we give it its life, which, in truth, it does not have. It is when we face our evil side, our fears, that we discover the illusion they are and take away their power and control over us. It is when we are willing to bring the darkness into the light that our light can transform the dark. We can not get rid of the dark by avoiding or denying its existence. So when we encounter someone we dislike, know that it is not them we dislike, but what they are showing us about ourselves that we dislike. The reverse is also true. When we encounter a person or something about a person we love, we need to know that they are just reflecting back to us that which we love about ourselves.

It is important that we bless each person and every situation that presents us this opportunity to see who we really are. Without these experiences we would have no way of knowing ourselves. Once we accept that everything we see in others is an aspect of ourselves, then we can choose if we want to continue to represent ourselves in this way. Once we have made our choice, then whatever it is about ourselves that is being shown to us no longer needs to be a part of our lives unless we choose it to be.

Do not forget we are here to reflect back to our creator the magnificence of its being through physicality. Each and every soul, every act—no matter how heinous—is a part or act of love blessed by our creator. We must recognize every person, every action as a divine act of love. This is truth. With this understanding we move up to the first stage of freedom, and that is the realization that we are love or God in action, and love is all that exists. Everything we do, or anything anyone does, is God expressing itself as love, and a declaration of the love that God has for itself, for his creations.

Now, if at anytime anyone uses this as an excuse for violence or abuse, then they do not know this as truth. If we held the realization that we are one as our truth, we would never abuse anyone because we would be abusing our self. We would not steal from others because we would be stealing from our self. We would not think of murdering another because we would be murdering a part of the totality of our being.

Until we can bless and love each and every aspect of ourselves, we will never know the truth of who we are. We will never know the joy of unconditional love or experience the peace that is waiting for us. Accept who you are and love all that is you. Decide how you want to represent yourself as the God that you are and all the joy, peace, happiness, and love you desire will be yours in the moment you call "Now."

Exercise: As you look out into the world, remind yourself that this world is one consciousness expressing itself in various forms, all of which are God, and each time you encounter another person(s) remind yourself that you are God and that you are encountering an aspect of yourself, another aspect of God. No matter what it is you like or dislike about the person, bless them for showing you an aspect of totality of your being. Judge the act not the actor. Ask yourself, "Is this is how I want to continue to represent myself in the future?" Then make a choice and live that choice. Even if you encounter people or events that you like or dislike through indirect ways such as the media, accept them as an aspect of yourself, of God, and bless them for what they are showing you about yourself. Then make your choice and be your choice.

CHAPTER 0 - 12

THE FINAL STEP:
OUR RETURN HOME

*When we see ourselves in everything
and everything as a part of us,
when we choose to surrender to our divinity,
then we become one with God and God is all that exists.*

The final step in the process takes place in the form of a healing. The healing is not in the form of a physical healing—although that can accompany the healing—but rather in the form of a spiritual healing. The timing of the healing, however, is out of our control. It is true that we must choose to be healed, but the actual time when the event takes place is up to our soul, which is God. Our Higher Self will decide when we are ready to return home. This is why the timing is different for every person.

There are many wonderful healing techniques and programs people are participating in to prepare for their healing. We are working on mending the relationships we have with our parents, our siblings, our spouse, and our inner child. However, the quickest way to facilitate the healing needed to bring us home is to evaluate and repair the relationship we have with God. This is our first and only true relationship. What are our core beliefs about God? Is God a punishing and vengeful God? Do we have to suffer and struggle as a way to atone for our sins? Is God a God of conditional love or unconditional love? It is in healing this one relationship that all our other relationships can be/will be transformed.

Who do we blame for the problems in our lives? We say we blame ourselves, our parents, our friends, but who even above these individuals do we believe is ultimately responsible for our lives? To whom is it that we pray? We do not pray to our parents or our friends. We pray to God. In the end, when all is said and done, it is God whom we believe is responsible for the circumstances of our lives. We blame God for the evil that exists in our lives and in the world. Until we have the courage to face God one to one and open our hearts to the truth, we will never know what the truth is. Not until we have the courage to face the wrath of our vengeful God will we discover that such a God does not exist.

When we reunite ourselves with the one mind of God, our creator, we face the worst fear of all: the fear of death. This can be the most frightening part of the whole process, although it does not have to be. When we die a physical death and leave this physical body, we do not rejoin God in heaven. We already are in heaven with God and always have been, we just forgot. Currently when we die, we just die into a different level of this same hallucination. We continue on in this same fantasy but without the density of this physical body. Until we decide to remind ourselves of who we are, we will not escape the veil of this illusion.

When we rejoin the one mind of God, we realize that we as a separate entity no longer exist. We understand that the body is an instrument of the soul, of God. Our physical existence is an illusion. The only death we ever truly have to encounter is a death in our own minds. Our death is actually a mental process where we kill our ego or divided self. We change our perspective from a separated individual self to a whole unified self. We understand that no one or no thing exists except for God, including ourselves. Once this is done, our current reality is totally reversed and the paradox is uncovered. We realize that death is actually and expansion of our self into a part of everything that exists. Death is nothing to be feared. It is a transition to a new life, to a new beginning.

We know we are nearing completion of this process when the veil placed between God and ourselves begins to fade away. We will have opened the doorway for our creator to take the final step in bringing us home. The God we created as judging, as punishing, as frightening, is destroyed. "How do we come to experience God as a totally loving and creative force?" The answer is, "When we realize and accept God as a totally loving and creative force." When we do this, we no longer view ourselves or our experiences as we did in the past. We realize every act we ever committed was an act of love. Also, any act we choose to or choose not to undertake will be an act of love. We forgive God for all that we considered as negative experiences in life and now bless God and thank him for our life. We understand the importance of each person and every event. We forgive ourselves for everything we have ever done and in this same instant we forgive everyone for anything they have done to us. We recognize every person and every experience as a loving part of ourselves and our creator. The veil between God and ourselves is gone. When we talk of God we are talking about ourselves. When we talk about ourselves we are talking about God. God does not exist separate from us. We are part of God. We have reminded ourselves of who we are and rejoined the whole. We have killed the old idea of ourselves and God. We have relinquished our individual separated ego self for our united Divine Self. Our life is no longer ours but God's.

The greatest paradox of life is that we have to go through an entire process where we reclaim our power, and then after reclaiming that power we must choose to surrender to that power. And the only way to surrender to that power is to become that power. So the power we are actually surrendering to is ourselves. In other words, the only way to be one with God is to accept that we are a part of God, and, in accepting that we are a part of God, we become one with God. We cannot be at one with something that we are not ourselves. In our surrendering we realize that this physical existence is not our true reality—it is a dream. We are part of a dream that we create but at the same time did not create. We can create our lives in any way we choose, but the choices we get to choose from are not our choice. They are determined by God and are limited by the unique expression of God we were created to be. It is as if we are all artists and we are each given different colors with which to paint. We can paint whatever we want with those colors, but we have only those colors to choose from. Then it is realizing that God is the paint, and that we are the paint. We are not what we paint. What we paint is of no consequence. Whatever we choose to paint, we are God expressing itself as love.

To better understand our lives and the enlightenment process, we need to understand that we cannot surrender something we think we do not have. We cannot choose to be something that we think we have no chance of being. That would be like promising a friend a million dollars when we know we only have a thousand dollars to give. It is only after knowing and accepting ourselves as powerful beings that we can choose to be those powerful beings. We can, however, deny our divinity as long as we like. We should remember, though, that our surrendering does come in the form of joy. When we surrender to our power, we choose to live life in such a way that we do only that which makes us feel good about who we are and expresses the kind of person we choose to be.

In our new enlightened state we are awake within the dream. We see the divine in everything. There are no accidents. Divine order is all that exists. God does not make mistakes. There is nothing to be feared. We do not need to choose love, we are love. Fear no longer exists. This does not mean that things we used to consider as negative or evil cease to exist, but that we see them as what they are—an expression of love.

In our new awareness we no longer concern ourselves with the particular circumstances of our lives. We advance to the highest level of freedom—a freedom which entails no choice. We have limited ourselves through our experiences to the point where we have no choice other than to be that one unique expression we represent of the Divine Whole. Everything is love and the only choice we have is to live our joy. We gladly give up our free will to gain our freedom. We no longer worry about our lives. We have total faith in our divine nature. The only concerns we have are those that surround developing the person we choose to be. We elect to focus on what makes us feel happy and joyful about ourselves and on the actions through which we are best able to express our joy.

What happens to God when our lives are joyful? The only time we seek God is when things go wrong or our lives are not the way we want. When we live life centered around our joy, we create a life of joy. Our life becomes a reflection of our joy, not the cause of our joy. We no longer need to seek God because we experience ourselves and everything as God. This does not mean that we no longer believe in a higher power, but that we exist as an expression of that power. God is not as some illusive force separate from us—we are a part of God. We do not concern ourselves with the past: it is merely what brought us here. It is not that we do not think about the past, but we do not dwell on it. It no longer controls us. Nor do we concern ourselves with the future. The future does not exist. All that matters is what makes us feel good now. It is in living our life in the now moment that we create the future. It is not that we do not make any plans, but that we are not attached to those plans. Life is meant to be a creative, joyful adventure. What would be the purpose of life if every day we could predict exactly what was going to take place? We can know that we will have all of our heart's desires and not concern ourselves as to how and when they will be manifested. This is what makes life interesting. It keeps the magic alive. As long as we trust in our joy, which is our connection to our Higher Self, we will be led to the life we were created to live. We will be expressing the unique part of God we were created to represent. It is in living our joy that we connect with our soul and the soul expresses itself. When we live out our soul's desires, we are making God flesh. When God is made flesh, God experiences itself and we experience our joy. Our will is God's will and God's joy is our joy. They are the same. We are the created and the creator. We are one.

The circle is complete. We are right back where we started. The circumstances of our lives may have not changed, but we have changed. We have given up our free will for our freedom. We have replaced our divided ego self with our unified Divine Self. Now we live a life rooted in love, not fear. We have remembered who we are and in our remembrance we regained our power. In surrendering to our power we become an expression of the God we used to seek.

This last exercise is very powerful and should not be undertaken lightly. It can lead to many changes and to unsettling circumstances in your life. Begin this process only after you have integrated the masters' principles in your life and you **feel** the time is right for you to begin this process.

Exercise: For three consecutive nights verbalize your intention to reunite with your Higher Self. The intention must be clear and spoken without any trepidation. Repeat this process every three months. Each time it is performed your soul will evaluate the request and decide if it is the right time for your atonement.

CHAPTER 0 - 13

THE METAPHYSICS OF OZ

No story more accurately portrays the enlightenment process than the story "*The Wizard of Oz.*" The entire story is symbolic of humanity's search for God. The story revolves around a young girl named Dorothy and her dog Toto and their magical trip to the land of Oz.

The story opens with Dorothy expressing her desire for peace and a place to live where dreams really do come true. The first step in the atonement process is choosing to remember who we are. She must make it known to the universe that she desires her atonement. This is evidenced in her singing the song "Somewhere Over the Rainbow." In the song she sings about heaven and makes it known to the universe that she desires a reunion with God. Once the desire is expressed she is, as we will be if we do the same, guided to the experiences which lead us to our awakening. Next, Dorothy decides that she must run away from home. If she does not leave home, her dog Toto will be taken away from her for trespassing on their neighbor's property. Dorothy's dog Toto represents the God-presence of love in our lives. It is no accident that dog spelled backwards is God. Dorothy's leaving home represents the level of commitment needed to find the God we seek. She loves Toto so much that she is willing to give up everything to save him. She would rather be with him more than anyone else. Likewise for our enlightenment, our desire to be with God must be so complete that we are willing to give up everything to be with him.

Running away, she meets a traveling man who convinces her to return home by tricking her into believing that her Aunt Emily is sick and misses her very much. Throughout our lives we meet many people and suffer much pain because we believe they have tricked and lied to us. However, the truth is that each person and every act is an expression of love. On her way back home a terrible storm erupts. When she returns to the house, she finds no one there. They have retreated to the safety of an underground shelter, and, because of the roar of the storm, they could not hear her pounding on the door. Unable to get in, she returns to her bedroom with her dog Toto, where she is hit in the head by a flying window and falls unconscious onto the bed.

She wakes up and discovers that they are in the house, whirling upwards inside a tornado, traveling somewhere over the rainbow. When the house finally lands, she opens the door and finds herself in Oz. Dorothy is in the heaven she has created in her mind. When we die a physical death, we do not return to God in heaven. We go to a place we create in our minds. It is just a different level of the same illusion we create here on earth. Appearing out of a beautiful ball of light, Glinda, the Good Witch of the North, comes to Dorothy. Glinda is Dorothy's Higher Self, or the

Holy Spirit, as it is called in the Christian religion. Glinda asks Dorothy if she is a good witch or a bad witch. Dorothy denies that she is any witch at all. Dorothy is actually denying her true power as a spiritual, creative being. When we refuse to accept who we are, we deny both our power and ourselves as a part of God. Dorothy is then informed by Glinda that when she landed in Oz, her house fell upon and killed the Wicked Witch of the East. The killing of the Wicked Witch of the East represents a step in Dorothy's atonement process. The awakening we seek is a process and not the result of a single event. Dorothy is hailed as a hero by the people of Munchkinland because they are free from the reign of the evil witch. She is hailed as a hero because, each step she makes in the process towards her enlighten-ment is an upliftment for the whole. Whatever we do on an individual basis affects the whole because we are a part of the whole.

Suddenly, out of a black cloud of smoke, the Wicked Witch of the West appears. Evil sister of the Wicked Witch of the East, she has come to find the one who killed her sister. The Wicked Witch of the West represents Dorothy's separated ego self: our dark side, our fears, our choice to live life refusing to accept who we are, veiled in an illusion of separation from God. The witch is reminded by Glinda of her sister's ruby slippers. When she goes to take them, they vanish and are placed by Glinda on Dorothy's feet. The ruby slippers symbolize the hidden power we have as a spiritual, creative energy. The red is symbolic of love, the source of our power and the path through which we will be led home to the remembrance of our divinity. When approached by the Wicked Witch, Glinda tells Dorothy to never give up the ruby slippers because they must contain great power, or the evil witch would not want them. She is instructed that if she ever gives the slippers away, she will be at the mercy of the Wicked Witch. When we give up our power we forget our connection to God, our source of love, and that is when we experience evil and live life in fear. Angered by the fact that she did not get the ruby slippers, the Wicked Witch threatens Dorothy and Glinda. Glinda laughs at the witch's idle threat, proclaiming that she has no power here, and, for her to leave before someone drops a house on her. Our Higher Self knows that the ego/fear is just an illusion and has no true power of its own. We in our belief in separation from God give the ego its power. After the witch leaves, Dorothy expresses her desire to get back home to Kansas. She is told that the only one who can possibly help her is the Great Wizard of Oz. The Wizard is Dorothy's God, our God. The Wizard lives in the Emerald City. The Emerald City is where God resides. The emerald is a symbol for beauty, wealth, and abundance. The emerald is a green stone and the color which in metaphysics is allied to the heart chakra.[5] It is through our heart that we find love and discover the path that will lead us back home to God. To get to the Emerald City she must follow the yellow brick road. The streets of heaven are paved with gold, and these

---

[5] Chakras are spiritual energy centers that are associated with different areas of the human body.

streets will lead us home to God. The riches we receive are lives of joy, peace, abundance, and love.

On her way to the Emerald City, Dorothy comes to a fork in the road. The forked road symbolizes that there is more than one path to a reunion with God, and no matter which path we take we are sure to get to heaven, because the ultimate reality is that we never really left heaven, we only think we did. At this junction she meets a scarecrow—a scarecrow in need of a brain. She releases the Scarecrow from the pole he is nailed to, and he decides to accompany her to the Emerald City in the hopes that the Wizard will give him a brain. Continuing on, they run into a rusted tin man in need of a heart. They oil the rusted Tin Man, and after oiling him they encounter the Wicked Witch. The Wicked Witch threatens to destroy the Scarecrow and the Tin Man if they help Dorothy reach the Emerald City. The ego, fearing its impending death, tries to stop the re-membering of our self, our remembering who we are. After the witch leaves, the Tin Man decides to join them on their journey to the Emerald City to help protect Dorothy and to seek a heart from the Wizard.

Along this path Dorothy is continually being confronted with experiences that challenge her current beliefs. Before we can uncover what the truth is, we must question all that we hold as truths about ourselves, God and the world we live in. We must open our hearts and minds to the possibility of a different truth before the truth of our existence can be made known to us. Dorothy confesses that she feels she has always known the Scarecrow and the Tin Man but she can not remember where or when. She wishes she could remember. It is in the remembrance of who we are that we reunite with the totality of our being and uncover the truth of our existence. When or where we gain our enlightenment is up to God, but we must walk the path to Oz as does Dorothy.

Finally, they meet a lion in need of courage. The Cowardly Lion joins the group to seek out the Wizard, who they are sure will give him some courage. The ensemble is complete. Dorothy has discovered the path home. She has re-membered all the aspects of herself needed for her enlightenment: the process of the mind, represented by the Scarecrow; the search for the heart or the path of love and joy, symbolized by the Tin Man; and the courage we need to undertake this process, represented by the Cowardly Lion.

When they spot the Emerald City off in the distance, they again cross the path of the Wicked Witch. It is in our experiences with fear or that which is not love that we come to know and define what love is. It is from this that we define ourselves. We must experience fear before we can make the choice for love. The witch casts a spell creating a beautiful field of poisonous flowers nearing the entrance to the city causing Dorothy, Toto, and the Cowardly Lion to fall asleep. Realizing that this is a spell cast by the Wicked Witch, and with nowhere else to turn, the Tin Man and Scarecrow yell out in desperation for help. Once we open our hearts and minds to the truth, we will no longer allow ourselves to stay asleep, veiled in the illusion of our current existence. Glinda appears and sends down a gentle snow undoing the evil witch's spell. Our Higher Self is always watching over us, and all we need to do is ask for help and know that it is on its way. Our dark side, our divided ego self, with seductions of beauty, tries to keep us asleep, veiled in the illusion. It is our Higher Self that awakens us to the truth. Upon waking, the heavens sing a song heralding Dorothy's forthcoming enlightenment.

When they reach the city, the guardian at the door denies them entrance into the city to see the Wizard until he finds out that Dorothy was sent by Glinda. The final step to our awakening is taken by God and occurs only after our Higher Self feels we are ready. After entering the city they are sent to clean up and prepare themselves for their meeting with the Great Oz. After they are cleaned up the Wicked Witch is spotted flying in the sky above the Emerald City. From the smoky exhaust of her broom, she spells out over the city the words "Surrender Dorothy." Once again Dorothy becomes fearful. It is in surrendering to our fears, not avoiding or denying them that we reclaim our power. It is through facing our fears head-on that we find the power to defeat our fears by discovering they are nothing but illusion. They run to the entrance of the Wizard's home, where they are again told by the guard at the door that the Wizard will not see them.

When the doorkeeper discovers that she is Dorothy of "Surrender Dorothy," he understands that it is time for her to face her God and goes to ask the Wizard if he will see them. The Wizard refuses. Dorothy begins to cry, and with this the guard begins to cry. He tells them that he will get them in to see the Wizard. It is through our heart, our feelings, that we open the door to our enlightenment and find our way to God. They are let in and walk down a long dark hallway. When they enter the main chamber, they are confronted by a large frightening male head which thunders out at them that he is the great and powerful Wizard of Oz. This is Dorothy's idea of God. The feared, all-powerful being represents the same God that has been created in our culture. They set forth their requests. He tells them that if they bring him the broom of the Wicked Witch of the West, he will grant their wishes. There is a task we must accomplish before we can rejoin the infinite mind of God and return home to a reunion with our Higher Self. The task we undertake is not some demand by God, not something we do to atone for our sins or earn our way back into heaven. It is a choice we make. Dorothy could have very well lived out her life in Oz. To get the broom she must confront the Wicked Witch. When we choose our awakening, we choose to confront our dark side, our ego self. We choose to face our fears and all the multifaceted aspects which we believe embody the entirety of our being.

On the way back to the witch's castle, Dorothy and Toto are captured in a forest by the witch's army and separated from the others. They are taken back to the witch's castle where they are held prisoner, locked inside a room. The Wicked Witch demands that Dorothy give her the ruby slippers. Dorothy remembers what Glinda the Good Witch of the North told her about giving up the slippers. Before she answers, the witch threatens to destroy Toto, so Dorothy agrees to let her take the slippers off her feet. When the Wicked Witch tries she fails and remembers that the only way she can remove the slippers is to kill Dorothy. Toto escapes from the witch's castle, and the Wicked Witch gives Dorothy one hour to live. Dorothy now faces the worst fear of all, the fear of death. But, we will see, it is in facing the fear of our own extinction that we discover everlasting life.

Toto returns to the forest to get the Scarecrow, the Tin Man, and the Cowardly Lion to save Dorothy. They return to the witch's castle where they unknowingly exhibit the characteristics they thought they lacked in order to save Dorothy from her death. The Tin Man cries at the thought of Dorothy in the witch's castle. The Scarecrow devises the plan to save Dorothy, and the Cowardly Lion is to lead the way. The Scarecrow, the Tin Man, and the Cowardly Lion become who they want to be because they love Dorothy. The irony in life is that we can not become the person we want to be unless we love ourselves for who we are now. In loving who we are now, we discover we are the person we always wanted to be.

Toto leads them back to Dorothy, and just in the nick of time they free her from her prison. On their escape from the castle they are trapped and surrounded by the witch and her army. The witch threatens to kill them all, leaving Dorothy for last so she can watch them die. The witch lights the straw of her broom and touches the Scarecrow on the arm, setting him on fire. Because of her love for the Scarecrow,

Dorothy searches for a way to save him and sees a nearby bucket of water. Dorothy grabs the bucket of water and throws it on the Scarecrow's arm, dousing the fire and splashing the witch. The water, the universal symbol for life, kills the witch by melting her. The task we must complete before we can receive our enlightenment is the destruction of our ego self. It is when we have the courage to face our ego self, our fears, that we discover the power to transcend our ego, to see it as the illusion it is. It is through the path of loving our self that we re-mind ourselves with the mind of God, re-member ourselves with God, and receive everlasting life. Again, Dorothy is hailed by the witch's army for killing the Wicked Witch. Each step we take in loving the totality of our being and re-membering our self, re-members the whole.

Dorothy, Toto, the Scarecrow, the Tin Man, and the Cowardly Lion return to the Wizard with the broom. The Wizard tells them to go away and come back tomorrow. Dorothy gets mad at the Great Oz and confronts him for not keeping his promises. The Great Wizard of Oz thunders at Dorothy for talking back to him. His wrath is made known. At this point they look over to a curtain that Toto is pulling back to uncover a man speaking into a microphone. Toto has exposed the Great Oz as a fraud. The Wizard is no more than a human like Dorothy herself. It is when we face the wrath of our angry God that we discover he does not exist. The God we thought of as God is no more than our self.

It is ironic that throughout the movie the Scarecrow, the Tin Man, and the Cowardly Lion exhibit all the qualities they think they lack. They just refuse to acknowledge them. In saving Dorothy, the Wizard makes them realize that they already have all the qualities they thought they were missing. Likewise, it is through loving the totality of all that we are and accepting ourselves as we are now that we discover the truth of our existence and everything we need at this very moment to return to a reunion with our creator. The Wizard presents the Scarecrow, the Tin Man, and the Cowardly Lion with symbols for what they thought they lacked inside. He gives the Scarecrow a diploma and the Cowardly Lion a medal of courage. While giving the Tin Man a ticking heart clock, he explains the paradox of life by telling the Tin Man to "remember, my sentimental friend, that a heart is not judged by how much you love, but by how much you are loved by others." We have been taught to believe that is by loving others before ourselves that we receive love, when the truth is, it is in loving ourselves first, before others, that we have love to give to others. So the only true measure of love is not how much love we **think** we are giving but how much love we **are** receiving.

When confronted with the problem of getting Dorothy home, the Wizard agrees to take her home himself in his balloon. He explains to them that one day he floated here in his balloon and from that day on the people crowned him "Oz, The Great Wizard Deluxe." The people of Oz, not the Wizard himself, created the image of the Wizard, just as we have created a God who is cruel, vengeful, and punishing because we accept that this is a part of who we are. When we have the courage to face this God, it is then that we discover he does not exist—that this is not a part of who we truly are. While preparing to take off, Toto spots a cat in the arms of a women and leaps out of the balloon. Dorothy jumps out of the balloon after Toto and the balloon takes off without her. (In following the path of love we remember who we are and discover the path home to God.) In retrospect we can see that it was by following the path of love, represented by her love for Toto, that Dorothy first left home and was led to Oz; agreed to give up her ruby slippers, which led her to having to face her own death; discovered the Great Oz was a human being like herself; and, after jumping out of the balloon to retrieve Toto, was, as we shall see, led to the remembrance of who she was and a reunion with God.

As Dorothy laments over the fact that she will never get home, Glinda the Good Witch of the North appears, telling her that she no longer needs any help to get home. Dorothy has reclaimed her power. Once we take back our power as a creative loving force, we open the door to the remembrance of who we are. Dorothy has remembered she is an expression of God. Glinda explains to her that she has always had the power to return home. However, if she had told her sooner she would not have believed her. She needed to learn it for herself. It was not enough for us to be told that we are God—we needed to experience it for ourselves. It is through focusing on our dark side that we come to know ourselves as light, as God.

Dorothy is asked what she has learned and she replies "It wasn't enough to just want to see Uncle Henry and Auntie Em, and if I ever go looking for my heart's desire again I won't look any further than my own back yard, because if it isn't there, I never really lost it to begin with." Glinda tells Dorothy that she is correct and with this knowledge she can return home. It is not enough just to want to be with God. We must realize that we are God, and if we ever go looking for God we should not look outside ourselves, because if God does not exist within us, God does not exist at all. We are the source of our own power. We return home when we choose to accept our divinity and stop searching for a God outside ourselves. (This is why the Great Oz floats away from the city because she no longer needs a Wizard—she is the Wizard.) Once we awaken the God within us, we will be a part of the God we used to seek. We will have remembered that we are an expression of God, and in doing this we become one with God, and God is made flesh. The Scarecrow tells Dorothy that this knowledge was so easy that he should have thought of it for her. The Tin Man feels that he should have felt it in his heart. It is as simple as choosing to remember who we are and having the courage to live our lives through our feelings of love and joy.

Dorothy then faces her sorrow in leaving the people she has grown to love. She says her good-byes to the Lion, the Tin Man, and the Scarecrow. She tells the Scarecrow that she will miss him most of all. In our remembrance we must be willing to give up the idea of an individual self. We will no longer exist as separate individuals. With three clicks of the heels of her ruby slippers Dorothy is on her way home. When she returns, she awakens in her bedroom, where she rejoins all the people she thought she left behind. She is told that her entire trip to Oz was a dream, that she never really left home. So too, when we complete our enlightenment we realize that this life we live is also a dream, an experience in the one mind of God. We do not leave this place or the people we love to return home because we, the collective we, were never gone in the first place.

We are all Dorothy, we all have Toto, and we are all wearing ruby slippers. Just as Dorothy was the dream and the dreamer, we are the created and the creator of this dream. Love is the reason we first decided to come here, it is the reason for all the experiences of our lives, and it is love that will get us back home. Our limited earthly existence is our Oz, and when we choose to remember who we are and follow the path of love, we will be led home to the place we never left.

CHAPTER 0 - 14

HINTS ON LIVING THE LIFE
WE WERE MEANT TO LIVE

Love thy neighbor as thyself.
If we do not love ourselves,
we cannot love our neighbor.
Loving ourselves is the greatest gift
we can give to ourselves and the world.

The Wizard of Oz ends with Dorothy awakening from her dream. This is not the end of her life, nor will ours end, when we awaken from the illusion of this reality. It is a new beginning. Every ending is a beginning and every beginning is an ending. Remember the circle. Love is the reason we are here, and it is in discovering that we are that love that we return home. Now that we have reclaimed our power and know that we are God expressing itself as love, it is our role to decide how we want to express our Godhead. When we awaken from the illusion of our current existence, we are at the point where we consciously co-create our lives with God. We do not live our lives based on what we were taught to believe, but by what makes us feel joyful and loving. We are no longer bound to our old ideas and beliefs about ourselves, God, and the world we live in. We choose to live life through the eyes of love and in the present moment. Our response to each experience is based on what gives us the most joy and makes us feel the most loving. It is not based on what we did in the past or what we expect to receive in the future.

The way to living the life we were meant to live is through the path of our heart, our feelings. This is how our soul expresses itself and makes itself known to us. It is in living our joy that we express the love that we are, and God is made flesh. The question for the newly enlightened soul is not whether or not it has choices, but, since all choices are a choice for love, which choice is the highest choice? The only person who can answer this question is the individual him or herself. Do not look to others for answers that only you have. Never give away your power. Listen to the voice within. The questions you need to ask yourself are, "What choice best represents the person **I** want to be?" "What choice brings **me** the most joy?" "Is this how **God** would act?" Answering these questions will lead you to the choice that is the most loving. The problem arises when we believe we can not distinguish between our desires and our wants or needs. Desires originate from our soul. They express the love that we are and lead us to experiences of joy, peace, abundance, and love.

Wants or needs, on the other hand, are ideas that our parents, our societies, our religions have taught us will bring us these rewards. Often, these teachings are contradictory, and we do not know which is correct. Today's society teaches that happiness is found in material success. Religion teaches that happiness is found in sacrifice and poverty. Which is correct? Which do you believe? We have in our society wealthy people that are unhappy and poor people that are unhappy. We have wealthy people that are happy and struggling people that are happy. So which is it? Can they both be correct?

To uncover our soul's desires we must question all that we hold as truth about ourselves, God, and the world. We must search our feelings to uncover what it is that truly expresses our joy. We should **not** question our feelings, even if what makes us feel good may not be considered "normal," because to question our joy lacks faith and trust in the intelligence of our creator and limits the expression of God as love. However, if at any time we use this as an excuse to do harm to another, we know that we are not in contact with our highest good.

There are simple guidelines to follow when seeking our desires and the fulfillment of those desires. A desire is first something that does not harm another living thing. Second, a desire is expressed in something that we need or is of value to us now. Third, a desire is something that makes us feel good—it expresses our joy. Joy is never the result of a desire, it is the cause. And fourth, a desire requires faith. How, when, or where our desire is going to manifest itself must be of no concern to us. To specify exactly how our desires should be manifested is to limit the expression of the desire, which is the same as limiting God. If what we seek meets these conditions, then we know that it is expressing our highest good and will be manifested in our lives through experiences of love, joy, peace, and abundance.

The path of the enlightened soul is learning to integrate and balance the totality of its being while existing within the paradox of being a spiritual being inside a physical universe, having to choose between good and evil, right and wrong, when no distinction truly exists, and trying to become something that we already are. Life is lived simultaneously on two levels. The first level is the level of "isness," which is who we truly are, a being of total love. In this level there are only absolutes, there are only love, joy, truth, abundance, and peace. There are no opposites. No separation exists. Everything is one and everything is love. Everything is God. However, on the second level, the physical level, the level of the illusion, everything is separate and nothing seems the same. In this illusion we are here to choose between good and evil, right and wrong, joy and sadness. We are here to choose either love or fear. We are here to experience both so we can choose how we want to recreate our Godhead, but at the same time we are not to condemn that which we do not choose. We are continuously involved in the act of creation—of creating ourselves anew each and every moment of every day from now on, just as is God. It is now up to us to choose if we will express God as the eternal, expanding, joyful, healing force of love or the controlling, judgmental, destructive force of fear. The choice is ours and always has been.

Since in the absoluteness of God there is no such thing as right or wrong, nor good nor evil, it becomes confusing for us as co-creators of our lives to choose how we want to express ourselves as love—since all actions are loving.

Many of the problems we experience today are a result of our inability to **decide for ourselves** what it means to be loving and how best to express the love that we are. However, to decide is what we must do, and in doing so we must define some things as not loving. But does our defining some things as not loving mean that they are intrinsically wrong or evil?

Many acts we consider non-loving are committed in the name of love, in the name of God: a spouse kills her mate for having an affair, or a doctor is killed for performing abortions. Are these acts of love? Is this how God would act? When we choose to awaken from this dream, the ego makes its last attempt to convince us that we are **the** enlightened one and that we have **all** the answers. The closer we get to our enlightenment, the more cunning and sly is the illusion of fear. Fear can disguise itself in acts we consider kind and loving. Remember, any act itself is neutral. It is the intent behind the act that determines its source. This was illustrated in the Wizard of Oz when the Wicked Witch cast a spell in the form of a beautiful field of flowers as Dorothy, and her friends neared the entrance to the Emerald City. The act appeared beautiful, but it was for a wicked purpose. When we accept our power and ourselves as a part of God, we must acknowledge that everyone else is also a part of God. We must never try to force our beliefs on anyone else. We must allow every person to choose how their divinity will be expressed.

In God there is no polarity; absoluteness is all that exists. However, within the current illusion of our physical existence, the nature of love appears to be constantly changing. The reason it appears this way to us is because we lack understanding of what love is. Love, which is who we are, is changeless. Because we lack clarity about the nature of love, I would like to discuss briefly some topics where the confusion surrounding love results in a great deal of personal pain and suffering and contributes to much of the negative energy in our society. My intent here is not to convince you that a particular view is correct, but to open your heart and mind to a greater understanding of the personality of the universe.

Is the life path of the enlightened soul a passive and defenseless one? When we choose to accept our divinity and be an expression of that divinity, does that mean we leave behind our physical lives? Do our lives become effortless. Should we reject society and go live out the rest of our lives chanting in some cave in the woods? Does an effortless life mean that all we do is sit in a chair meditating for what we want and then wait for a knock on the door? Or does it mean that when we choose to consciously express our divinity, in whatever form it may take, that we begin to see the harmony in the events of our lives, and that even though it may require a great deal of effort, to do it bring us so much joy that it seems effortless?

Is the millionaire whose life is lived by doing only what she wants and whose life requires little physical effort expressing her divinity more than a struggling artist who works two jobs just to support her art? Is the person who struggles with their life, constantly examining him or herself and seeking truth but passing up the experience of this physical existence expressing their divinity more than the person whose life is spent actively pursuing happiness with little or no time spent on self-reflection? Does it have to be one way or the other, or is it possible to have it both ways?

Before you decide, let me remind you that this physical universe was designed as both a vehicle through which we could **choose** how we want to express our divinity and as a way for us to **experience** that choice.

When we choose to be an expression of love, does this mean that we become a doormat and let everyone walk all over us? Is it the irony of our lives that there are times when we must give up our image of who we should be, to be the person we want to be? Is love only expressed in those acts we consider loving? Is it loving to stand idly by, watching our family being murdered at the hands of an intruder, leading the intruder to believe by our inaction that murder is acceptable? Or is it more loving to kill the intruder, preventing him from killing our family, and thereby making it known by killing him that it is wrong to terminate another life? However, this type of reasoning should **never** be used as an excuse to justify murder or harm another living thing. The decision to harm someone or end their life should never be made out of a desire for revenge or punishment. The only time the experience expresses love is while the act is being committed. Only then does the experience open the person's mind to the possibility of a new belief. To harm or kill another person for any reason other than self-preservation is to state to the universe that brutality and killing is acceptable. Remember, in God there is no past or future; the only time that exists is the present. So, any act committed as revenge or punishment for an act committed in the past or motivated by a future consequence is fear-based, because the past and future are illusory concepts.

The relationships we have in life are the most important aspect of our lives. They are the foundation of our very universe. Without these various relationships we would have no way of defining ourselves.

Does the success of a relationship depend on making the other person(s) happy? Or is it in making ourselves happy that we create successful relationships? If love is the reason we stay with someone who is abusing us, then what does this say about how we feel about ourselves? Is this love or fear? "If someone you loved were to give up their happiness for you, would that make you happy?" Or, is this what tears at the very fabric that holds the relationship together?

We constantly try to change the context of our relationships by trying to change the other person(s) involved, when the only person we have the power to change is ourselves. Remember, everything in life is a reflection of ourselves. Trying to change any part of our lives by altering the outward symbols of our lives would be like trying to change how we look by altering the mirror we look in. This is why we encounter the same type of relationships over and over. Until we realize that the person we need to change is our self, the type of relationships we create will be the same regardless of who the participants are.

In relationships should we seek what we believe is lacking in ourselves and our lives, such as love, money, power, security, and sex, or should we seek to share that which we already have? Should the goal of every relationship be to make the other person(s) involved dependent on us for their survival? Or, should the goal of every relationship be to help the person(s) involved become independent, to reclaim their power, so they can then choose if they wish to stay in the relationship and share the person they have become with one another?

The way we can begin to change all the unhappy relationships in our lives can be revealed to us when we begin to understand and accept the purpose we have given to the relationships in our lives. The question we must ask ourselves is, "Were relationships designed as the way through which we become whole, and it is in finding that special person(s) that we can feel happy and complete, or were relationships created as a vehicle through which we express/experience our completeness and our happiness?"

Since God is omnipotent, omniscient, and unlimited possibility, would the expression of these qualities best be demonstrated in a physical universe through a narrow and limited presentation of Self or through an unlimited and multifaceted exhibition of Self? If God is everything and all that exists, is there anyone or anything that can not be a part of God? If we wanted to glorify the unlimited magnificence of our being, would there be only one expression of that magnificence? Is it possible for any person to be less than or better than anyone else, or any race to be less than or better than another race, or any society or culture to be less than or better than any other society or culture?

What type of being would be reflected in a world where everyone looked the same, acted the same, and thought the same? Remember, we are the body of God, here to express the magnificence of its being. Prejudice does not exist in our lives as a result of our encounters with people. Prejudice exists in our lives to reflect back to us our own prejudice. So the question we must ask ourselves is, "Are we here to define and limit the expression of God into a singular expression of this force, or are we here to experience, love, and honor all our differences because they reflect the many faces of God?"

At the highest level we are not heterosexual, homosexual, or bisexual. We are not physical beings, we are spiritual beings. Sexuality is a means of expressing the love energy, and that expression takes on many forms. The act of sex is a physical manifestation of our desire to be one with God, our creator. If we relate the act of sex to our numeric analogy, humanity is represented by the number one, and God is represented by the number zero. Sexual intercourse is the insertion of the one into the zero, or the desire of humanity (one) to be inside or one with God (zero). The sex act, whether it be vaginal, oral, or anal, between men and women, between men, between women, or with oneself, is an acting out of this desire to be one with God. This is why the sexual desire is so strong. Also, this is why the act of sexual intercourse can produce life—spiritual life, not physical life. Through the marriage of our masculine, rational, physical side with our feminine, intuitive, spiritual side, we obtain life. When we remember who we are, we reunite with our creator, uncover the illusion of our current existence and discover everlasting life.

Sex is to be an exchange, a feeling experience between consenting individuals who come together in a union of love to express feelings of joy. Remember, the soul is after a feeling experience, and the universe does **not** recognize any union as more sacred than any other in its desire to obtain this feeling. This union between souls can be the greatest experience of God we can have while on this plane of existence. So as long as love is being expressed, does it make any difference as to what form the expression of this love takes? Or, is it our role to limit the expression of love and choose only one way that love should be expressed for all individuals?

Many religious philosophies teach poverty and sacrifice as the way to salvation. However, if God is a loving God and we are his children, is this what we think he would wish for us? Is it the wish of every parent for their children to struggle, suffer, and live in poverty?

To obtain the salvation we seek, must we overcome this physical world by denying its reality and the pleasures it can offer us, or is it that we just need to overcome our attachment to them? If we are poor and have few material possessions does this guarantee us a spot in heaven, and does a person of wealth have little or no chance of obtaining salvation? Is it part of the paradox of our lives that if we try so hard to deny or overcome this earthly existence, that this very act will actually keep us bound to this physical existence and prevent our salvation? What if the wealth we obtain is a reflection of our feeling abundant and not the source of our wealth, then can we have all the abundance the universe has to offer us?

Are the riches we seek found outside of us? Is true abundance a feeling or is it measured by the amount of material possessions we have? Is the person who outwardly has little in the way of material possessions but is grateful for all that she has, more or less well off than the person who has great material wealth but inwardly feels that whatever she obtains will never be enough? You must ask yourself, "Who has the greater peace?" "Which person would I rather be?"

It is in focusing on the person we want to be and expressing that person that we express our love and find the peace, joy and abundance that is waiting for us. When we express our soul's desires, the entire universe supports us in our efforts, and we will be successful.

There are circumstances in our lives that we willingly create and others that we draw to us. Either way, all of our experiences are a result of our thoughts and therefore they are our creations. The peace, happiness, love, and abundance we seek is not in creating any specific circumstances in our lives but in our response to the circumstances we create. We have to ask ourselves, "What is the purpose of my life?" Is life to be about who we are or what we do? "Make **yourself** your career, not the work you do." There is a plan for our lives—a plan that has been planned for us, that we have planned, and that we are planning. It is in surrendering to this plan that we express our divinity and experience the love, joy, peace, and abundance that is the universe. Remember, love is all that exists. Fear is an illusion. The only thing we can call *evil* is that which prevents us from living the life we were created to *live*. And the only thing that can prevent us from living this life is fear. **Trust in the plan**. **Live your joy**. We need to stop trying to force our happiness by creating a life that we think will make us happy, when we should be following what makes us happy and letting our lives develop naturally from the pursuit of our happiness.

We create our lives but we did not create life itself. There was a purpose for our creation. We must never forget that we are a part of something that is much larger than each one of us. It is when we can totally **surrender** and **trust** this force that we find the peace we seek. We do not have to worry about being let back into heaven because we were never cast out. What we have to do is to wake up to this truth. We are at the point of our evolution where we have the experience of ourselves, but we lack remembrance of who we are. Our adventure in fear has served its purpose. It is now time for us to make our choice. Will it be fear or love? It is up to us. It is time for us to choose to remember who we are, accept our power as creator, and set free that unique expression of God we were created to be. We are here to live out our greatest potential, and in order for us to live this potential, we must surrender ourselves to God. It is time to remember with God and awaken from this dream. Accept that you are an expression of God. This is who you are now and always have been. In acceptance of this is your salvation.

BIBLIOGRAPHY

The following is a list of books that provided the inspiration and foundation for much of the material contained within this book. If you wish a more detailed discussion on the ideas embodied in this book, I suggest you seek out and read the following books.

Carey, Ken. *The Starseed Transmissions*. New York, NY: Harper Collins Publishers, 1982.

Elkins, Rueckert, McCarty. *The Ra Material*. West Chester, PA: Whitford Press, 1984.

Foundation for Inner Peace. *A Course in Miracles*. Glen Ellen, CA, 1975.

Kirkwood, Annie. *Mary's Message to the World*. Grass Valley, CA: Blue Dolphin Press, 1991.

Kryon. *The End Times Book I*. Del Mar, CA: The Kryon Writings, 1992.

Kryon. *Don't Think Like a Human Book II*. Del Mar, CA: The Kryon Writings, 1994.

Patent, Arnold. *You Can Have It All*. Piermont, NY: Money Mastery Publishing, 1984.

Roberts, Jane. *The Nature of Personal Reality*. Englewood Cliffs, NJ: Bantam Books, 1974.

Rodegast, Stanton. *Emmanuel's Book*. New York, NY: Bantam Books, 1985.

Rodegast, Stanton. *Emmanuel's Book II*. New York, NY: Bantam Books, 1989.

Walsch, Neale Donald. *Conversations with God*. Norfolk, VA: Hampton Roads Publishing Co., Inc., 1995.

Wapnick, Gloria/Kenneth. *The Most Commonly Asked Questions About A Course in Miracles*. Roscoe, NY: Foundation for A Course in Miracles, 1995.

A FINAL QUERY

If you cannot accept yourself as a part of God,
then how can you ever become one with God
if God exists as someone or something
separate from yourself

?

Ordering Information

Additional copies of this book can be ordered directly from the publisher.

OBODONI PRESS
P.O. Box 409036
Chicago, IL 60640-9036

(773) 506-1070 • FAX (773) 506-2044